HW

■ DRUGS
The Straight Facts

Anti-Anxiety Drugs

DRUGS The Straight Facts

Alcohol

Alzheimer's and Memory Drugs

Anti-Anxiety Drugs

Antidepressants

AIDS Treatment Drugs

Birth Control Pills

Body Enhancement Products

Cocaine

Date Rape Drugs

Designer Drugs

Diet Pills

Ecstasy

Hallucinogens

Heroin

Inhalants

Marijuana

Morphine

Nicotine

Opium

Prescription Pain Relievers

Ritalin and Other Methylphenidate-Containing Drugs

Sleep Aids

DRUGS
The Straight Facts

Anti-Anxiety Drugs

Donna Toufexis and
Sayamwong E. Hammack

Consulting Editor
David J. Triggle
University Professor
School of Pharmacy and Pharmaceutical Sciences
State University of New York at Buffalo

CHELSEA HOUSE
PUBLISHERS
An imprint of Infobase Publishing

Anti-Anxiety Drugs

Chelsea House
An imprint of Infobase Publishing
132 West 31st Street
New York NY 10001

Library of Congress Cataloging-in-Publication Data

Toufexis, Donna, 1959–
  Anti-anxiety drugs/Donna Toufexis & Sayamwong E. Hammack.
    p. cm.—(Drugs, the straight facts)
  ISBN 0-7910-8556-2
  1. Tranquilizing drugs—Juvenile literature. I. Hammack, Sayamwong Emwill.
II. Title. III. Series.
RM333.T68 2005
615'.7882—dc22   2005021243

Text and cover design by Terry Mallon

Printed in the United States of America

Bang 21C 10 9 8 7 6 5 4 3 2 1

This book is printed on acid-free paper.

All links and web addresses were checked and verified to be correct at the time of publication. Because of the dynamic nature of the web, some addresses and links may have changed since publication and may no longer be valid.

Table of Contents

The Use and Abuse of Drugs

The issues associated with drug use and abuse in contemporary society are vexing subjects, fraught with political agendas and ideals that often obscure essential information that teens need to know to have intelligent discussions about how to best deal with the problems associated with drug use and abuse. *Drugs: The Straight Facts* aims to provide this essential information through straightforward explanations of how an individual drug or group of drugs works in both therapeutic and non-therapeutic conditions; with historical information about the use and abuse of specific drugs; with discussion of drug policies in the United States; and with an ample list of further reading.

From the start, the series uses the word *"drug"* to describe psychoactive substances that are used for medicinal or non-medicinal purposes. Included in this broad category are substances that are legal or illegal. It is worth noting that humans have used many of these substances for hundreds, if not thousands of years. For example, traces of marijuana and cocaine have been found in Egyptian mummies; the use of peyote and Amanita fungi has long been a component of religious ceremonies worldwide; and alcohol production and consumption have been an integral part of many human cultures' social and religious ceremonies. One can speculate about why early human societies chose to use such drugs. Perhaps, anything that could provide relief from the harshness of life—anything that could make the poor conditions and fatigue associated with hard work easier to bear—was considered a welcome tonic. Life was likely to be, according to the seventeenth century English philosopher Thomas Hobbes, *"poor, nasty, brutish and short."* One can also speculate about modern human societies' continued use and abuse of drugs. Whatever the reasons, the consequences of sustained drug use are not insignificant—addiction, overdose, incarceration, and drug wars—and must be dealt with by an informed citizenry.

The problem that faces our society today is how to break the connection between our demand for drugs and the willingness of largely outside countries to supply this highly profitable trade. This is the same problem we have faced since narcotics and cocaine were outlawed by the Harrison Narcotic Act of 1914, and we have yet to defeat it despite current expenditures of approximately $20 billion per year on "the war on drugs." The first step in meeting any challenge is always an intelligent and informed citizenry. The purpose of this series is to educate our readers so that they can make informed decisions about issues related to drugs and drug abuse.

SUGGESTED ADDITIONAL READING

David T. Courtwright, *Forces of Habit. Drugs and the Making of the Modern World.* Cambridge, Mass.: Harvard University Press, 2001. David Courtwright is Professor of History at the University of North Florida.

Richard Davenport-Hines, *The Pursuit of Oblivion. A Global History of Narcotics.* New York: Norton, 2002. The author is a professional historian and a member of the Royal Historical Society.

Aldous Huxley, *Brave New World.* New York: Harper & Row, 1932. Huxley's book, written in 1932, paints a picture of a cloned society devoted only to the pursuit of happiness.

David J. Triggle, Ph.D.
University Professor
School of Pharmacy and Pharmaceutical Sciences
State University of New York at Buffalo

Introduction

I had always hated elevators. Every time the door closed I would wonder if I would ever see daylight again. I still used to get in them though. At least I did until that day last winter.

Concordia University's main building is 13 stories high. Almost everyone uses a series of escalators to get up to the floor they want. The Biology department is on the 12th floor and so people studying or working in that department are basically the only ones using the two small elevators located on the first floor to get up there. I used to go up in the escalators every morning. One Friday morning in January, I had just come inside from a frightfully cold winter's day. I was late so I decided to take the elevator upstairs. There were three of us in the elevator that day: myself, a young woman who must have been studying engineering because she pressed the 9th floor button to get off on the Engineering and Mathematics floor, and an older man dressed in scrubs who I recognized as being one of the Animal Care personal.

I pressed the button for the 12th floor and the doors closed. As I said, I was always a little nervous in elevators so I watched as the light for each successive floor lit up as we ascended. Third and fourth floor and so far so good. Five and six and going strong. Then just as we passed the 7th floor, the elevator came to such an abrupt stop that the three of us simultaneously lost our balances. Then it jerked a few more inches upward and one side seemed to get stuck. It stopped again, this time with one side of the elevator a few inches higher than the other side. The three of us stood on the higher portion of the floor and faced towards the incline in order to stop ourselves from slipping. The older man pressed the alarm button and waited. No one answered. He pressed it again. The same silence. He then started pressing the open door button. The door opened slowly. A wall made of concrete bricks faced us. We realized then that we were lodged in, stuck like mortar between the 7th and 8th floor.

It was at this point that I began to feel panic. My heart seemed to be racing uncontrollably. The pounding in my ears was all I could hear, and nothing else in the little room seemed to matter. My hair stood on end as the fear gripped me. The walls seemed to be closing in around me. I was losing control of my body, and I thought that I might die. Each second of fear seemed to make things worse. The blood drained from my face and I felt like I would pass out any second. I would die in there with no food, and even worse, no water! I started to scream "Help, help!' The other people in the elevator tried to calm me down. "What do they know," I said to myself. They are going to die also. I pushed them away. Just then a voice came through the intercom. "We'll get you out," it said. Then the elevator shuddered from side to side and finally started to move upwards once more. It opened on the 8th floor and all three of us rushed out. After that terrible panic attack, I never got in that elevator again. And I never will.

Donna Toufexis
Spring 1992

1

Fear and Anxiety

WHAT IS FEAR?

Most people feel scared at different points in their lives, and fear is one of the most recognizable of emotions. In fact, many of us are frightened almost daily, by events such as being late for an exam, talking in front of a large group of people, or walking down a dark street. Fear has been programmed into our bodies, and serves an important purpose. It coordinates our actions in the face of threat (Figure 1.1).

The threatening events that cause us to be scared fall into two classes: those that are **innate** (i.e., we are born with them) and those that are learned. We seem to have an innate sense of fear to some situations—that is, we are sometimes scared of things even if we've never experienced them before or if they have never threatened us in the past. For example, many people are afraid of the dark, even if they have never had a bad experience in the dark. Some scientists believe that we have an innate fear of certain shapes, like the shape of a snake.

Alternatively, many of the things that scare us are things that we have learned are threatening. Consider flying in an airplane in the months following the September 11th attacks in New York and Washington, D.C. Even experienced travelers felt a high level of anxiety when flying in an airplane after those events. Many of us still have a heightened sense of anxiety in airplanes. Most of the things we fear fall into the category of "learned fears": We are generally scared of people, places, and things with which we have had, or have observed others having, a bad experience.

OCTOBER 22, 2001

www.time.com   AOL Keyword: TIME

AFGHANISTAN: INSIDE THE GROUND WAR

TIME

THE FEAR FACTOR

Anthrax letters. FBI warnings. Bin Laden's videotapes. Bombarded by threats real and imagined, a nation on edge asks, What's next?

$3.95US
44>
0 925679 8

Figure 1.1 Fear is part of our everyday lives. Due to the events of this century, the psychology of fear is playing an even larger part in our politics and in the media. This *Time* magazine cover represents the fear that erupted over the events following the September 11, 2001, attacks on the World Trade Center in New York and on the Pentagon in Washington, D.C.

What is the purpose of fear? First, fear is a motivation. We tend to avoid situations that scare us. For example, when we are walking through the woods, we might avoid areas of tall grass and dense shrubbery, out of fear of stepping on something we cannot see. Likewise, we may have a tendency to fear unfamiliar places. Although we try to avoid these situations, we are still sometimes faced with a proximal, or close, threat.

What happens when you are faced with something close and threatening, like an angry animal or a nearby automobile that is out of control? Your body changes. Your face might turn pale. Your hair might stand on end. You might start breathing more quickly. You might feel extremely hot or extremely cold. These are all consequences of physiological reactions that prepare you to deal with a threatening situation in which you might be injured. Your skin goes pale because fear makes your blood vessels constrict, so that blood is channeled away from your extremities and toward your skeletal muscles, thus preparing you to fight or to run. Your hair stands on end as your body tries to conserve heat that will be lost as your blood vessels constrict (this is why you might "shiver with fear"). Your breathing becomes rapid to provide your brain and muscles with more oxygen. In addition, more sugar is released into your bloodstream, also to be used by the brain and muscles. You become aroused, and your senses become more acute.

Scientists call these physiological changes the "fight or flight" response, because their purpose is to prepare the body to either face the threat or leave the situation. This response can be observed in most animals, and therefore is considered a highly adaptive defensive mechanism (Figure 1.2). That is, fear is an important emotion for our survival.

But what happens when the fear system breaks down? A person might no longer feel scared in a threatening environment. This type of malfunction is rare, but it happens. What

Figure 1.2 Cats and other animals have a physical response to fear that scientists consider a highly adaptive defense mechanism. The arched back, flattened ears, and raised hair on the cat's body are designed to intimidate a potential threat or attacker.

is much more common is the opposite situation in which the fear system turns *on* at inappropriate times. In some instances, the fear system becomes overly activated in response to certain stimuli, so much so that it dramatically affects the lifestyle of the afflicted person. These instances fall under the categories of phobias and panic disorders. In other situations, fear systems are activated even when the stimulus is unclear, or there is a malfunction in the process of turning the fear system off, so that the person is chronically afraid. These instances fall into the general class of anxiety disorders.

HISTORY: ANXIETY

Although anxiety disorders were officially recognized by the American Psychological Association (APA) in 1980, reports of the occurrence of anxiety disorders can be found throughout recorded history. Such prominent figures as Isaac Newton, Emily Dickinson, Abraham Lincoln, and Sigmund Freud all suffered symptoms that would now be classified as an anxiety disorder.

In the 1500s, the term *hysteria* was used to describe anxiety-like afflictions. One of the first English accounts of hysteria was written by the physician Edward Jorden in 1603. Jorden believed that the women who were accused of witchcraft were actually afflicted with what he called "hysterical" illness. He was often called as an expert witness for the defense in witchcraft trials, but was not always persuasive.

In the late 1600s, Thomas Willis coined the term *neurology* and suggested that hysteria was a disorder of the nerves and brain. Willis was an important figure in establishing the biological bases for psychological disturbances.

Reports of hysteria continued for the next several hundred years. The term *anxiety* was coined by the second half of the 17th century, and was used in medicine to explain restlessness and some conditions that resembled what we would today call panic attacks.

Up to the late 1800s, each symptom of anxiety was treated as a separate physical complaint and believed to be caused by problems in the heart, ear, gut, and brain. First, Bendedict-Augustin Morel suggested that the symptoms of anxiety resulted from a common source, a neurosis, which is a problem in the brain. Around the same time, the ear-nose-throat doctor Maurice Krishaber suggested that anxiety symptoms were a disease of the cardiovascular system. Several others suggested that some of the symptoms described by Krishaber were in fact due to problems with the inner ear.

In the 1890s, Sigmund Freud defined *anxiety-neurosis* as a clinical condition that was rooted in a psychological problem. Thus, Freud suggested that the many physical symptoms we now know as anxiety, which had previously been treated as separate ailments, were actually the result of one psychological (subjective) cause, which he called "anxiety-neurosis."

In the early 20th century, more was being written about cases that would be classified as anxiety disorders today. The French psychiatrists Ludovic Dugas and Paul Hartenberg each wrote books that described social phobias. Hartenberg suggested that timidity was due to fear, shame, and embarrassment in social situations. Around the same time, also in France, Francis Heckel wrote a description of what we call "panic disorder" today, and analyzed its relationship to other anxiety problems, including generalized anxiety, obsessions, and phobias.

In the 20th century, many milestones were reached to establish psychology, psychiatry, and neuroscience as the formal practices that they are today. During this time, the study of anxiety disorders was developed into its current state. Notable events include Austrian-Hungarian endocrinologist Hans Selye's (Figure 1.3) pivotal work on the stress response in the 1930s. Selye did much to define how we think about stress and its effects on the body, and how the stress response can lead to illness.

Motivated by the mental health problems of returning soldiers from World War II in 1946, the National Mental Health Act gave the surgeon general the authority to promote mental health through research. This law led to the creation of the National Institute of Mental Health (NIMH) in 1949.

Figure 1.3 Hans Selye was a pioneer in the field of stress research. He systematically studied the stress response and defined how we think about stress and its effects on the body.

In 1952, the American Psychological Association created the first *Diagnostic and Statistical Manual of Mental Disorders* (DSM-I). This book was the result of a four-year effort to develop a standard national naming system for mental disorders. It is updated regularly, and remains the standard by which mental illnesses are defined today.

Also in the 1950s and early 1960s, **serotonin** and **dopamine** were discovered to be **neurotransmitters** (later we will explore how these neurotransmitters are targets for anxiety-reducing drugs). Moreover, research into the first antidepressant drugs was suggesting links between neurotransmitters and mood. As the first drugs became available for treatment of mood and anxiety disorders, drugs for mental health became a big business in the United States. In fact, since the 1960s, the history of anxiety and fear disorders has become dominated by research into the drugs used to treat these disorders.

HISTORY: ANTI-ANXIETY DRUGS

Drugs are chemicals that are used for their effects on bodily processes. Many drugs have been found to alleviate the symptoms of fear and anxiety. Currently, the drugs that are used to treat anxiety disorders have been carefully examined in controlled studies and shown to be more effective than placebo. (Placebos are fake pills that the patient does not know are fake. Often, placebos can also have beneficial effects in mental disorders.)

Historically, alcohol has been used as an anxiety-reducing agent, both casually and in professional medical settings. In 1903, barbital was introduced as the first **barbiturate** to treat anxiety, and phenobarbital followed a few years later. Barbiturates have many side effects and addictive properties, and overdose can lead to coma and death. For these reasons, they are rarely used today, except to treat some forms of epilepsy. This class of drugs was eventually replaced by the **benzodiazepines** (see Chapter 4).

TYPES OF ANXIETY DISORDERS

As we discussed earlier, fear is an adaptive response to threatening situations, and is manifested by several changes in the body that function to prepare the body to fight or to flee. These changes include the constriction of blood vessels, piloerection (your hair stands on end), rapid breathing, and arousal. As we begin to discuss fear and anxiety disorders, it will become clear that most of these disorders involve either the presence of fear and these bodily changes in inappropriate situations, or an inappropriate magnitude of these responses to a fearful stimulus.

Phobias

The word *phobia* comes from the Greek word for "fear," *phobos*, and refers to an inappropriately intense and irrational fear toward some object or situation. Most adults who experience phobias recognize that the fear is irrational. Most phobias fall into the category of specific (sometimes called "simple") phobias. The more complex social phobia (also called "social anxiety disorder") will be discussed later.

Specific phobias come in many forms but can be categorized into these general categories:

1. **Animal phobias**: These often involve an intense fear of spiders, snakes, rodents, dogs, or any other animal stimulus. Although there is some natural and adaptive inclination to be scared of spiders, snakes, and certain other animals, since they might be poisonous or pose some other health threat, the phobic person has an *extremely* intense and inappropriate fear of these stimuli. The person might exhibit fear responses simply when he or she imagines the stimuli. The person will take extreme precautions to avoid encountering these animals. For example, a person with a phobia of snakes might refuse to go hiking or even to walk around a grassy backyard.

Seeing a captive snake behind glass at a zoo might produce a severe physiological fear reaction in phobic individuals, while most of us recognize that such a situation is not dangerous, and do not experience a fear reaction.

2. **Environmental phobias**: Some common environmental phobias include the fear of heights and the fear of water. Again, these are persistent and irrational fears that might make someone unwilling to walk out onto a pier for fear of falling into the water and drowning. The person might be aware that the water is just a few feet deep, and that the feelings of fear are irrational, but will still feel an intense motivation to avoid the situation.

3. **Situational phobias**: A common situational phobia is the fear of flying. The fear of flying is often *not* a fear of crashing, but rather a fear of being trapped in a small space and losing control. Phobias are often fairly specific, so that even if someone climbs mountains and has no general fear of heights, he or she may have a very strong phobia of escalators or elevators. Remember that an important descriptor of phobias is that they are *irrational*, given the situation.

4. **Blood and injury phobias**: Many people have injection phobias, and these phobias usually begin at very young ages. Like all the fears we have described, injection phobias are very pervasive, so that people who experience them might avoid ever going to the doctor for fear of getting shots. Likewise, some people have a persistent dental phobia, or fear the sound of the dental drill.

Around 6.3 million adult Americans are affected by specific phobias, and as many as one in 10 people will experience a specific phobia at some point in their lifetime. Moreover, phobias affect twice as many women as men. Thus, phobias represent one of the most common anxiety disorders.

Causes

The causes for specific phobias are not well understood. Because phobias have a specific stimulus, many researchers have argued that learning systems within the brain produce these pathological reactions to the feared target. In one of the more famous studies in the field of psychology, learning theorist John B. Watson showed that fear could be learned through experience. Watson presented a white rat to an infant boy, which did not produce any noticeable fear in the baby. However, Watson subsequently made a loud noise (like crashing pots and pans together) whenever he presented the rat to the child. Later, when he showed the rat (without the noise) to the infant, the baby cried and behaved as if he were afraid of the rat.

Based on Watson's study, psychologists have suggested that phobias stem from a previous pairing of the feared stimulus and an aversive event. Although this may be true in many cases, there are some reasons why this may not be the best explanation. First of all, many phobic individuals cannot remember the initial event from which their phobia stems. Instead, they might say, "I've always been afraid of snakes." This might suggest that, in fact, there *was* no initial event, that the person was born with the phobia. While this might be true, psychologists sometimes argue that the initial event may have happened at such a young age that the person simply isn't able to remember it consciously, but the learned association is still there subconsciously.

Another reason why this idea might not be a perfect explanation involves a learning process called **extinction**. When two events are paired together (as in the case of the rat and the loud sound), humans and animals can learn that one event (the rat) can predict another (the loud sound) and thus develop a fear of the rat. However, when the events are subsequently presented alone (the rat without the loud sound), the fear diminishes over time through a process called extinction. Extinction does not work well with phobias. That is, simply presenting the feared object in a safe environment does not reduce the fear as quickly as would be expected if the phobia were simply a learned fear. Again, psychologists have suggested that if the learning event took place when the brain was still developing (when an individual was very young), then the learned phobia might be much harder to change once the brain has matured.

Treatment

Much phobia treatment involves **behavioral therapy**, which involves working with a therapist to try to reduce fear of an object through the use of particular exercises, often without using drugs. Extinction is the natural process by which exposure to a feared object in a safe environment reduces the fear of that object over time. It is thought that part of the reason extinction does not work well with phobias is that phobic people are rarely presented with the feared stimulus in a safe environment, since phobias lead to avoidance behavior. Often, behavioral therapy involves exposing the individual to the stimulus (or parts of the stimulus) until the fear is reduced. These sessions can last a few months.

If the phobic individual suffers a debilitating anxiety, anti-anxiety drugs can be prescribed to alleviate these symptoms. We'll discuss the available drug options in detail in later chapters.

Panic Disorder

Panic disorder is characterized by the repeated and often unpredictable occurrence of **panic attacks**. According to the *Diagnostic and Statistical Manual of Mental Disorders*, panic attacks have an abrupt onset, reach their peak in 10 minutes, and are accompanied by at least 4 of 13 listed symptoms, which include shortness of breath, increased heart rate, chest pain, dizziness, choking sensations, numbness or tingling, hot/cold flashes, sweating, trembling, and nausea. Victims of these episodes feel an intense fear that can be better characterized as terror, often of losing control of their body and/or mind, and thoughts of death. Notably, the stress of one panic attack can often lead to excessive worry that eventually brings on further attacks.

The prevalence of panic disorder in the United States has been placed between 1.5% and 3.5%. Most of these cases are found in young adults, and panic disorder is very rare in the elderly. In addition, panic disorder tends to affect twice as many women as men, with more than 70% of panic disorder diagnoses occurring in women.

For victims, panic disorder tends to last a long time. Studies that followed patients with panic disorder found that after six to seven years, most patients still experienced panic attacks and were still taking medication to treat their

AN ESCALATOR PHOBIA

A phobia is an inappropriately intense and irrational fear toward some object or situation. The fear is overwhelming, causing both emotional and physical reactions. This testimonial was given by an employee at the State University of New York in Binghamton, New York, who had a specific situational phobia.

When I was a six-year-old, I fell down an escalator the way someone might accidentally fall down a half flight of stairs. I have a very vivid memory of having parallel, bloody scrapes down the front of my legs. Despite this, I was a resilient child and I was back on escalators within the day. My phobia began a few years later. I was playing at the top of an escalator with my brother. My shoe became caught in the escalator and I was thrown off balance. I was in midair when my brother grabbed my T-shirt and saved me from the fall. But from that moment on, I feared escalators. Thinking about riding an escalator led to that same rush of adrenaline and symptoms. One-quarter of these patients reported little improvement after six to seven years of treatment. Because panic attacks can feel like heart attacks or strokes, victims are likely to seek immediate treatment, and thus health care costs are estimated to be higher for panic disorder than for other anxiety disorders.

Studies of patients with panic disorder suggest that those who suffer from panic report having quality of life as poor as that of patients with major depression. Panic attacks and/or fear of panic attacks can interfere with the development of social relationships, personal happiness, and employment. The inability to hold a job can have a severe impact on the patient's financial independence. Up to 60% of patients

that same fear of falling. I wouldn't even eat at the food court because the sight of the escalators nearby would make me nauseous. But, I guess as far as phobias go, I was pretty lucky. Since exposure to an escalator is predictable, they are easy to avoid. I simply became one of those people who always took the stairs at the airport and the mall. When I did ride escalators, I would break out in a sweat, feel my heart race, and feel extremely woozy. Usually, if I tried hard, I could keep my composure. But in some instances, the only way to prevent myself from crying was to sit down on the escalator steps or make a companion stand directly in front of me to block my view (and potentially break my fall). Needless to say, I was given some strange looks. It is hard to explain how threatening a set of moving stairs can seem. But the metal tooth-like stairs of an escalator couldn't have looked more ominous and its flimsy sliding handrail brought me no reassurance.

diagnosed with panic disorder also develop depression, and these patients are faced with an even smaller probability that treatment will be effective and a greater chance of developing more severe anxiety symptoms.

Mechanisms

If your relatives have panic disorder, then you potentially have a greater risk for developing the disorder. Studies of twins and families with panic disorder show that you have a 10% risk of developing panic disorder if your parents were diagnosed, compared with a 2% risk of developing the disorder if they were not. Thus, there is a strong genetic component to panic disorder.

In 70% of patients with panic disorder, injecting sodium lactate, a chemical that is produced in muscles when there is not enough oxygen in the blood, produces panic attacks. The mechanism behind this effect is still poorly understood. In addition, rapidly increasing levels of blood carbon dioxide can trigger panic episodes. These consistent findings have led scientists to propose that the brain is sensitive to signs of suffocation in patients with panic disorder, leading to inappropriate alarm with modest changes in blood levels of lactate and carbon dioxide.

Within the brain, panic disorder has been associated with multiple **neurotransmitters**, including **GABA**, serotonin, nor-epinephrine, and corticotropin-releasing hormone, which is a stress hormone. Several brain areas have also been implicated in the development of panic attacks, because different manipulations in those areas produce or reduce panic-like behaviors in laboratory animals. For example, activating an area of the brain called the dorsomedial hypothalamus produces what looks like a panic attack in rats. Moreover, injecting the stress-associated corticotropin-releasing hormone into the **amygdala** can increase the sensitivity of rats to other manipulations that produce panic attacks, like lactate injection.

Benzodiazepines act by increasing the ability of GABA to inhibit cells in the brain. Since benzodiazepines are effective in treating anxiety disorders, scientists have suggested that decreased GABA function in areas such as the amygdala may cause anxiety-like symptoms. Reducing GABA function in the amygdala increases the sensitivity of rats to panic attacks, as corticotropin-releasing hormone does.

Treatment

Although scientists have investigated many drugs for the treatment of panic disorder, both the benzodiazepines and **antidepressants** have been shown to be the most effective. The choice and regimen of treatment is often determined by the possibility for drug interactions and other problems that might occur. Importantly, some evidence suggests that cognitive-behavior therapy is also effective in treating panic disorder, even when drugs are not used for treatment. Currently, the effectiveness of cognitive-behavior therapy as opposed to drug therapy is a controversial topic, but both remain viable options for patients with panic disorder.

Benzodiazepines

A multitude of studies show that benzodiazepine is effective in the treatment of panic disorder, sometimes freeing patients from panic attacks after six to eight weeks of use. Benzodi-azepines tend to work quickly, with a reduction in panic being observed as little as one week after the start of treatment. However, benzodiazepines have the risks of tolerance and dependency. Common benzodiazepines used to treat panic disorder include alprazolam (Xanax) and clonazepam (Klonopin).

Alprazolam (Xanax, Xanax XR)

Typical starting doses for the treatment of panic disorder are 0.5 mg of Xanax three times a day. Xanax can also be found in an extended release capsule called Xanax XR. As with all of the benzodiazepines, tolerance and dependence are important issues to consider when taking these drugs (Figure 1.4).

Clonazepam (Klonopin)

For the treatment of panic disorder, the starting adult dose is 0.25 mg twice a day, which may be increased by one mg daily after three days. Clonazepam's safety and effectiveness has not been determined for individuals under the age of 18. Side effects in the treatment of panic disorders are similar to many of the benzodiazepines, and include allergic reaction, inflamed sinuses or nasal passages, flu, menstrual problems, respiratory infection, speech problems, and vaginal inflammation.

Antidepressants

Antidepressants are as effective as benzodiazepines in the treatment of panic disorder. Moreover, antidepressants do not have the same risks of tolerance and dependency that are associated with benzodiazepine treatment. However, antidepressants take longer to work, so that significant improvement might not be observed until after a month of treatment. Although tricyclic antidepressants have been approved for the treatment of panic disorder, the effectiveness of selective serotonin reuptake inhibitors (SSRIs) in its treatment has led them to become the favored treatment among antidepressant drugs.

Paroxetine (Paxil, Paxil CR)

For the treatment of panic disorder, the usual starting dose is 10 mg a day (12.5 mg for Paxil CR). Side effects can include anxiety and nervousness (usually at the start of treatment and going away after a few weeks), tremor, trouble sleeping, weakness, nausea, diarrhea, constipation, weight loss, dry mouth, headache, sweating, trouble urinating, and decreased sexual drive. Side effects that are less common include muscle pain, breathing problems, chills, fever, and mood swings.

Alprazolam (Xanax)

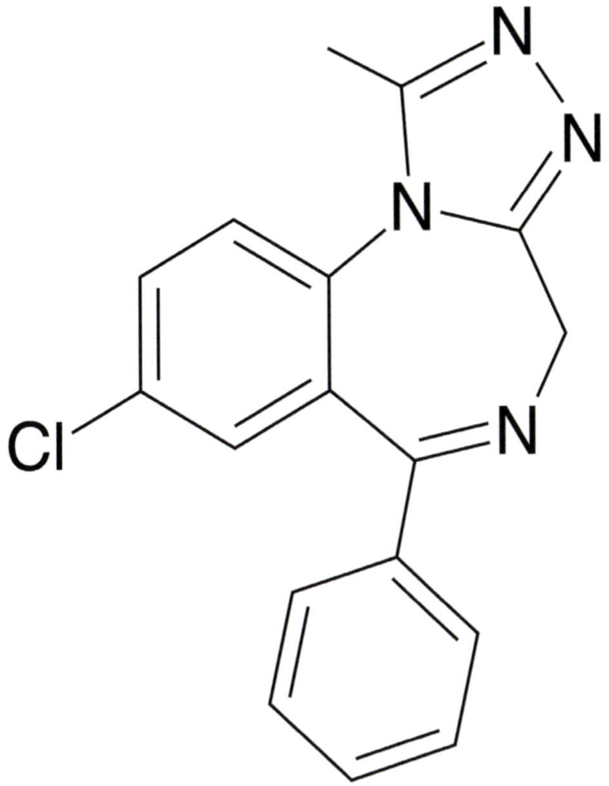

Figure 1.4 The chemical structure of alprazolam (Xanax) categorizes the drug as a benzodiazepine. Treatment with benzodiazepine is recommended for patients with panic disorder. Xanax can be habit-forming and treatment should be closely monitored by a physician.

Fluoxetine (Prozac)

Although fluoxetine is prescribed for people as young as eight years old for the treatment of depression, doses for the treatment of panic disorder have not been determined for those under the age of 18. For the treatment of panic disorder, fluoxetine is usually started at 10 mg per day. Doses can be increased or decreased depending on the individual circumstance. Side effects are the same as those described above for paroxetine.

Sertraline (Zoloft)

For the treatment of panic disorder, sertraline is generally started at 25 mg per day for the first week, and subsequently increased to 50 mg once a day as needed. Side effects are the same as those described above for paroxetine.

Benzodiazepines or Antidepressants?

There are advantages and disadvantages with each of these classes of drugs. Benzodiazepines are quick acting, but can have acute side effects, including drowsiness and fatigue and a decrease in coordination and cognitive function. Moreover, benzodiazepines carry a strong risk for physical dependence, as tolerance develops with long-term use, and the quick termination of treatment can be associated with withdrawal. Antidepressants also have side effects and must be administered for several weeks before they begin to be effective, but they are not associated with a risk for physical dependence and are effective in treating a broad spectrum of mental problems. Because panic disorder often occurs along with other mental disorders, such as depression, antidepressants are often the best form of drug therapy. One drug can act on several different but related problems. It should be noted, however, that benzodiazepines are not as effective in the treatment of depression.

SOCIAL ANXIETY DISORDER

Social anxiety disorder (also called "social phobia") stems from the fear of doing something wrong and being embarrassed in

A PANIC ATTACK

Panic attacks are episodes of very obvious physical sensations. Each episode produces a fearful state that can make the patient more sensitive to future episodes. This is called a "positive feedback loop," where one event increases the likelihood of a second event, which increases the likelihood of a third event, and so on. Here is one firsthand account of a panic attack.

> It was the evening after a really stressful oral exam, and I was talking on the phone. I don't know why, but part of my body seemed to go numb, and I just sort of freaked out. It was like the realization that I had no control over the part of my body that was going numb was so intense that my brain couldn't handle it. I ran into my mom's room, but I was having these flashes where I felt really hot and a little dizzy. Eventually she calmed me down, but there was a five- or ten-minute period where I was so scared that I was losing my mind. The problem was, with each flash I was getting more and more freaked out, because I thought that I was going to completely lose control of my body. I probably had 10 or so flashes, and each one made me more and more scared.

> When I think about that episode, what is scariest is how physical and real the sensation was. I mean, I really felt the numb, prickly sensation like when your leg starts to fall asleep. And I really felt hot. It wasn't like I was in some dreamlike state. I was awake and alert, and if I knew then what I know now about heart attacks and strokes, I would have been fairly certain that's what was happening to me.

front of other people. Many people are shy and get embarrassed easily in front of others, but for most of us, this shyness doesn't prevent us from entering a social environment. Patients with social anxiety disorder find social situations so unpleasant that they tend to isolate themselves, avoiding social situations whenever possible. When these people are confronted by a social situation, they often show physical reactions, such as blushing, tremor, and panic attacks. These physical symptoms reinforce their avoidance of social situations.

Social anxiety disorder is related to panic disorder in that panic attacks often accompany the symptoms. However, social anxiety patients only have panic attacks in particular social situations; the attacks do not occur spontaneously when the patient is alone or sleeping.

Some victims of social anxiety disorder are only afraid of specific social situations. These individuals might be capable of enjoying a conversation with friends over lunch, but the thought of giving a speech in front of a group of people can cause them to experience panic-like symptoms. This type of social anxiety disorder is called "nongeneralized" or "specific" social anxiety disorder. Some of the more common specific fears include public speaking, eating in public, using public restrooms, and being the center of attention in a group. Other people are deeply afraid of all social situations, whether it is a small group at work or an auditorium full of people. This form of the disorder is called "generalized" social anxiety disorder.

In the United States, 13% of people will be diagnosed with a type of social anxiety disorder at some point in their lifetime. As with many of the anxiety disorders, women have a greater chance of being diagnosed (16% for women versus 11% for men). Like panic disorder, 57% of patients with social anxiety disorder have another anxiety disorder at the same time. Of these, 37% also have depression, and 15% have a drug dependence.

Mechanisms

Much like panic disorder, there is a genetic link to social anxiety disorder that increases the risk of developing the disorder if your parents have developed it.

Research into the biological mechanisms behind social anxiety disorder has suggested that the two different forms (generalized and nongeneralized) may result from problems in different brain systems. The nongeneralized or specific form of the disorder tends to be more sensitive to agents that target norepinephrine beta receptors, which affect the autonomic nervous system (one aspect of the stress response). Not surprisingly, these individuals show a heightened autonomic stress response when in the environment that they fear. By taking a medication that suppresses this response (a class of drugs called **beta blockers**), these individuals can sometimes overcome their fear and perform in that particular social situation.

The generalized form of social anxiety disorder, on the other hand, is thought to be due to problems with dopamine and serotonin systems. Interestingly, people with Parkinson's disease, which is characterized by low levels of dopamine, are more likely to develop generalized social anxiety disorder. Also, a malfunction in the dopamine system has been shown to make it more likely for a person to have a detached personality, which is a characteristic of patients with social anxiety disorder. Serotonin systems are thought to be involved because SSRIs are effective in treating this form of the disorder. Although these systems have been implicated, little is known about how they are malfunctioning to produce the symptoms that characterize this problem.

Treatment

The treatment of social anxiety disorder is less established than that for other anxiety disorders. Different reports present conflicting findings about the effectiveness of the drugs commonly used to treat other anxiety disorders. Also, treatment is made more difficult because the different forms of social anxiety disorder seem to be the result of different mechanisms in the brain.

As with panic disorder, cognitive-behavioral therapy is an important part of the treatment program for social anxiety disorder. Some evidence suggests that in some cases, drug treatment did not improve the effects of receiving cognitive-behavior therapy.

Beta-blockers

As mentioned earlier, people with the nongeneralized specific form of social anxiety disorder can be helped by taking beta-blockers immediately before they have to face a feared event (such as giving a speech). Propranolol is a common beta-blocker that can be given at doses of 10–40 mg before the activity and will help suppress fear-like symptoms such as sweating and shaking. Controlled studies show that this class of drugs can benefit nongeneralized specific social anxiety disorder. However, research has also shown that these drugs do not appear to be effective in treating the generalized form.

Benzodiazepines
Alprazolam

Although alprazolam is effective in the treatment of panic disorder, research has shown mixed results as to whether this drug can be effective in the treatment of social anxiety disorder. Although some studies have shown that alprazolam is not any better than the placebo, some have also shown that alprazolam can reduce some of social anxiety disorder symptoms.

Clonazepam

Where the effectiveness of alprazolam for social anxiety disorder is unclear, evidence suggests that clonazepam is very be effective. Of patients given 0.5 to 5 mg per day of clonazepam, 85% showed a marked improvement in their social anxiety disorder. However, because of the side effects and risk of dependency associated with these drugs, the benzodiazepines are not commonly prescribed for social anxiety disorder.

Antidepressants

In the case of social anxiety disorder, research suggests that some of the antidepressants that are effective in other anxiety disorders do not work to ease the symptoms of social anxiety disorder. This is true of the tricyclic antidepressant imipramine and fluoxetine (Prozac). The first line of treatment for the generalized form of social anxiety disorder is an SSRI such as paroxetine or sertraline.

OBSESSIVE-COMPULSIVE DISORDER

Obsessive-compulsive disorder (**OCD**) is a condition marked by constant intrusive thoughts and irresistible time-consuming behaviors. It is quite rare, occurring in only about 1.9% to 3.3% of the general population. A person with OCD experiences repetitive unwanted thoughts, called obsessions. These obsessions produce feelings of impending disaster and urgency that require the person to enact repetitive and often ritualistic behaviors known as compulsions. OCD is grouped into five main categories based on the type of obsession that occurs. One type is called a "somatic" obsession. In this type, a person believes that something bad is happening to his or her body. For example, the person might be convinced that bugs are crawling just beneath the skin, even if they can't easily be seen. This obsessive belief causes a compulsion of checking and rechecking the skin. The person must repeatedly find the time and the privacy during the day to make sure that his or her skin is not infested.

The most common type of OCD is an obsession with contamination that leads to compulsions for cleaning the environment and washing any areas of the body, like the hands or face, that might become contaminated. A person with this kind of OCD often has the compulsion to wash his or her hands over and over again, even if the skin becomes chapped, red, and bleeding.

In another kind of OCD, the person becomes obsessed with having an orderly environment. For example, things must be arranged symmetrically in their rooms. Books must be grouped according to size or thickness on their shelves. There must be exactly seven steps from the bed to the door, and these must be counted exactly each time the trip is made. These types of OCD symptoms are grouped together and returned to as symmetry obsessions with counting or ordering compulsions.

Hoarding things is another example of OCD. People with these symptoms obsessively collect things, like newspapers or bottle tops. They cannot bear to part with any part of whatever they are collecting. They are consumed with obtaining the next part of their collections. They have difficulty thinking about anything else.

The last category of OCD includes people who have sexual or religious obsessions and compulsions. People with the religious type of OCD might believe that something bad will happen to them or a loved one if they do not constantly repeat a particular prayer. Someone with a sexual obsession may believe that they will not be able to engage in sexual activity unless they perform some ritual, like repeating a song lyric, at least 100 times a day.

There are also some disorders that are believed to be related to OCD because they include similar types of behaviors or are thought to affect the same areas of the brain. These are labeled OCD spectrum disorders. They include hypochondria, Tourette's syndrome, trichotillomania, pathological gambling, and kleptomania. Hypochondria is a consuming preoccupation with fears of having a disease, which persists even when the person is assured by doctors that nothing is wrong. It is related to OCD because of the uncontrollable thoughts that something is wrong. Tourette's syndrome consists of motor tics, or sudden jerky movements. Often, a person with Tourette's syndrome will laugh or swear for no apparent reason. Tourette's is believed to be related to OCD because OCD symptoms occur in about 30 to 60% of people who have Tourette's. Trichotillomania is the compulsion to pull out one's hair. People suffering form this usually start by pulling out the hair on their scalps but eventually, if the disease is not brought under control, they will pull out all the body hair they can reach. Syndromes like pathological gambling and kleptomania (compulsive stealing) are classified as impulse disorders related to OCD. In these conditions, an individual cannot resist the impulse to gamble even if he or she stands to lose an important relationship or food money. In kleptomania, a person cannot resist the urge to steal even if it means being arrested.

As you can imagine, OCD is one of the most debilitating of the anxiety disorders. Moreover, its symptoms usually get worse over time until the patient spends a great part of the day thinking about obsessions or enacting compulsions.

Mechanisms

As with most other anxiety disorders, the cause of OCD remains far from certain. There seems to be a genetic factor that makes people more likely to develop OCD because first-degree relatives (that is, people like siblings and parents) of patients who have OCD show a statistically increased rate of OCD-type symptoms even if they do not experience the full-blown version of the disorder. Also, studies of identical and fraternal twins show that where one twin has OCD, the other twin has a 67% chance (for identical twins) and a 31% chance (for fraternal twins) of developing the disorder.

Conditions in the immune system also seem to play a role in OCD. This connection arose because the development of a movement disorder called Sydenham's chorea, which occurs in children following a particular type of bacterial infection that causes rheumatic fever, also often produces obsessive-compulsive behaviors.

Although the cause of OCD is unknown, there are several brain areas that are believed to play a role in the development of the disorder. Most of these candidate areas have been implicated in OCD through what are called "imaging studies." Imaging studies are done using new technologies, including functional magnetic resonance imaging (fMRI) and positron emission tomography (PET) to take a picture of a person's brain. These images can show which brain areas are active or, perhaps, under- or overactive in people who have specific disorders like OCD. Images from people with OCD show that regions of the frontal cortex (which is involved with thought and decision-making) are overactive, and other parts are underactive compared to the same regions in normal people. Again, as with several other anxiety illnesses, it is difficult to determine if these changes in brain activity happen *before* the onset of the disorder or are caused *by* the pathology.

Treatment

In most cases, SSRIs are the first choice for drugs to combat OCD. Clomipramine, fluvoxamine, fluoxetine, paroxetine, sertraline, and citalopram are all SSRIs that have been proven effective in reducing OCD symptoms. However, in about 40 to 60% of patients, these drugs do not completely alleviate all the symptoms. When this is the case, a second type of drug called a "neuroleptic" is often added. Neuroleptic drugs, such as haloperidol, clozapine, risperidone, and chlorpromazine

are chemicals that act on neurons that release the neurotransmitter dopamine. A large number of these dopamine
neurons are located in the frontal lobe of the brain that, as we
have seen, is the area implicated in the development of OCD.
Neuroleptics reduce the amount of dopamine that these
neurons release. The fact that the combination of a neuroleptic with an SSRI reduces OCD symptoms suggests that
frontal lobe systems that use both dopamine and serotonin
are malfunctioning in OCD.

A Specific Animal Model for OCD

An animal model with the complicated name "schedule-
induced polydipsia" is specifically thought to resemble OCD.
The word *polydipsia* means "to drink" (*dipsia*) "many times"
(*poly*). Researchers discovered that if rats were restricted
to eating on a very fixed schedule, they would drink more
water than normal. This increased drinking is thought to be
a compulsive behavior that reduces the stress of the food
restriction. Rats undergoing this treatment reduce their excessive drinking when they are given SSRIs, which is why this
model is thought to resemble OCD. It may not be exactly like
OCD, however, because rats that are given benzodiazepines
will actually *increase* their drinking even more. In any case, this
treatment is the only animal model available at the present
time believed to resemble OCD.

POST-TRAUMATIC STRESS DISORDER

Post-traumatic stress disorder (called PTSD for short)
occurs following the experience of a severe threat to life or
physical well-being. People most commonly associate experiences during war with the development of this disorder in
soldiers. However, many other traumatic events can lead to
the development of PTSD. In fact, more women than men
suffer from PTSD (despite the fact that more men than
women become soldiers).

Although it is estimated that 61% of men and 51% of women experience at least one serious traumatic event during their lifetime, the incidence of PTSD in the general population is only about 7%. This suggests that certain people are particularly vulnerable and that there may be a preexisting condition that leads someone to develop PTSD. Indeed, much of the current research under way on PTSD is focused on individual differences in factors such as the hormonal response to stress that may incline someone toward acquiring this illness.

The symptoms of PTSD are divided into three main types, and a person diagnosed with PTSD will have experienced these symptoms for at least one month. The first is intrusive reexperiencing of the traumatic event. This means that the individual cannot escape from thoughts and memories of the incident. Circumstances that occur in everyday life bring to mind vivid, unwanted memories that remind the person of the event. For example, one combat veteran from the Vietnam War described being in a restaurant where someone was frying pork. The odor of the pork, a common food in Vietnam, made him feel as if he was in immediate danger. His physical reaction, which included sweating, rapid heartbeat, and fear, made him feel like he was back in combat.

The second major symptom of PTSD is an active and persistent avoidance of anything associated with the trauma. This means that the person avoids anything that can possibly be connected with the context in which the trauma took place. In the example of the Vietnam veteran, the former soldier went out of his way to avoid going outside if the ground was wet on a summer day, because such conditions reminded him of the Vietnamese jungle. Similarly, he avoided contact with anyone of Asian heritage who would remind him of the native people in Vietnam. Another component of this second set of symptoms is emotional blunting. That is, things that would make an unaffected person recoil, such as the scene of a fatal car accident, or things that would elicit an emotional response, such as the news that someone is seriously ill or has died, bring no response at all from someone with PTSD. Because of this, people with PTSD often have a range of social problems and difficulty interacting with friends and family members.

The third major symptom of PTSD is a state of perpetual physical and psychological arousal. It is as if the fear network of the brain, which includes the amygdala and other regions that we discussed earlier, is constantly active. People with PTSD are always vigilant and on the alert. They have trouble relaxing and their sleep is often severely disrupted.

Because of this range of symptoms, people with PTSD find it very difficult to maintain jobs or relationships. They often abuse alcohol or other mood-altering drugs to help them deal with their symptoms.

Mechanisms
People suffering from PTSD frequently have abnormal levels of the hormones that are involved in the body's response to stress. Studies have shown that baseline cortisol levels in people with PTSD are lower than normal, and epinephrine and norepinephrine levels are higher than normal. However, it is not known whether these differences in hormones and neurotransmitters involved in the body's stress response precede or follow the development of the disorder. It is important to note that the neurotransmitter and hormone changes seen with PTSD are separate from, and actually opposite to, those seen in major depression. In major depression, cortisol levels are elevated and epinephrine and norepinephrine levels are low. The distinctive profile associated with PTSD is also seen in individuals who have both PTSD and depression. One hypothesis is that people who cannot mount a robust stress

hormone response in reaction to a traumatic event are those who will ultimately acquire PTSD.

Thyroid function also seems to be enhanced in people with PTSD. Again, it is not known if this occurs before or after the onset of symptoms. It is known that thyroid hormone enhances the activity of serotonin, which, as we have seen, is the neurotransmitter most critically involved with maintaining a positive mood. It is possible that people who develop PTSD are those with dysregulation of serotonin neurotransmission.

It has been shown that after stress or injury, the brain produces and releases its own natural version of opiates to control pain and ease anxiety. People with PTSD continue to produce elevated levels of natural opiates after the trauma has passed. In addition, there exists an increased use of heroin and other opiate-based drugs of abuse among patients with PTSD. Once more, it is difficult to determine whether these elevated natural opiates existed before the disorder developed.

PTSD is linked with the increased likelihood of other psychiatric disorders occurring at the same time. Some 88% of men and 79% of women with PTSD meet the criteria for another psychiatric disorder. The most common disorders that men have at the same time as PTSD are alcohol abuse or dependence (51.9%), major depressive episodes (47.9%), conduct disorders (43.3%), and drug abuse and dependence (34.5%). The psychiatric disorders that most frequently co-occur with PTSD in women are major depressive disorders (48.5%), simple phobias (29%), social phobias (28.4%), and alcohol abuse/dependence (27.9%). These statistics may indicate that people with PTSD are more susceptible to psychiatric disturbances in general.

Although there are several physiological differences among patients with PTSD, it is difficult to tell whether any of them were present before the onset of the illness and are, therefore, involved in the development of the condition.

Consequently, the only certain cause for PTSD is the exposure of a vulnerable individual to a severe trauma.

Treatments

The most effective drugs for controlling PTSD are the SSRIs. It is interesting that, despite the fact that all SSRIs work by approximately the same mechanism, there are differences in the way particular SSRIs affect the symptoms of PTSD. For example, two different large-scale studies found that the SSRI fluoxetine controlled the patients' overreactivity and heightened arousal, and reduced the feeling of emotional numbness, while the SSRI sertraline, which also reduced emotional numbness, improved avoidance behavior but did not affect emotional arousal. This probably means that although both of these drugs act to block serotonin reuptake they likely have other, not well-understood effects that lead to slightly different treatment outcomes.

In addition, there are other types of drugs that work better than SSRIs in some PTSD patients. One of these is a class of drug called "tricyclic antidepressants." The name comes from the three-ring structure of the drug. These drugs block the reuptake of the neurotransmitter norepinephrine. Like serotonin, norepinephrine is released in brain areas that help control aspects of emotion. However, whereas serotonin is thought to be mostly involved in controlling mood, norepinephrine is more involved in systems that control the brain's level of arousal, or how attentive a person or animal is to its environment. Recall that one of the major symptoms of PTSD is being overly aroused and unable to feel calm. Tricyclic antidepressants often act as serotonin reuptake inhibitors also, and perhaps it is because they increase levels of both norepinephrine and serotonin that they are effective treatment for some people with PTSD.

Another type of drug that has proven effective for some PTSD patients includes compounds called MAOI, or MAO inhibitors. The letters *MAO* stand for "monoamine oxidase." Monoamine oxidase is an enzyme (a chemical that causes a reaction to occur between two other molecules) that exists inside some neurons. It causes the breakdown of the neurotransmitters dopamine and norepinephrine. If this enzyme is stopped or inhibited (the *I* in *MAOI* stands for "inhibitor"), then the neurotransmitters are left intact and can continue to affect neuronal firing rates and so on. The fact that MAOIs work in some patients with PTSD also suggests that norepinephrine and perhaps dopamine are important in reducing symptoms of this illness.

An Animal Model for PTSD

Because PTSD results from the experience of a severe trauma, scientists attempt to create this condition in a rodent model using a very harsh technique, but one that has produced some of the symptoms in rats that are seen in people with PTSD. Rats are placed in a large container of deep water from which there is no escape. After the rat has swum around for five minutes, a net is used to hold the rat underwater for 30 seconds. Rats that undergo this treatment all show elevated acoustic startle for the first few days following this harrowing experience. The acoustic startle response is a reflex that happens when a sudden loud noise causes certain skeletal muscles to contract, resulting in a jumping motion. You have probably experienced this response when someone sneaks up behind you and shouts "Boo!" The acoustic startle response is useful for measuring anxiety and fear because it is greater when a person or animal is in a fearful or anxious state. By about a week after the water experiment, the acoustic startle response of most of the rats returns to normal, but there are always a few rats whose acoustic startle response remains high even three weeks after the event. It is these animals that are believed to experience PTSD. Once you have produced these vulnerable rats using this treatment, you can then ask what is different about the brains of these animals that is causing them to have this symptom of PTSD.

GENERALIZED ANXIETY DISORDER

If you could summarize the symptoms of **generalized anxiety disorder** (**GAD**) in one word, the most appropriate word would likely be *worry*. People who suffer from this type of anxiety disorder spend much of their time worrying about things that may be about to go wrong. For example, someone with GAD may be consumed with anxiety over the state of his or her finances, even when it is obvious that the person is not in debt or facing any impending financial crisis. A person with GAD might constantly worry about the health and safety of a loved one, and even constant reassurance that that person is fine does not relieve the feelings of anxiety. Indeed, patients with GAD often describe themselves as being slaves to worry.

GAD differs from other types of anxiety disorders because, although the anxiety is present most of the time, GAD patients do not fear specific events such as social situations or having a panic attack (as in social anxiety or panic disorder). GAD is distinguished from normal worry or anxiety because of its long-term duration. GAD is frequently the underlying cause of many symptoms, including irritability, insomnia, headache, and muscle tension. This can often make it very hard to diagnose. A person with GAD will often go to his or her family physician and complain of "nerves."

GAD affects about 4 million Americans. It usually manifests after childhood and before a person reaches middle age. It happens about twice as often in women as in men. Symptoms must persist for at least six months before a diagnosis of GAD may be made. In addition, GAD often occurs along with other psychiatric illnesses, such as depression or bipolar disorder, or with drug abuse, which probably leads to an underestimation of the amount of people affected by this disorder. There is some evidence that the disorder has a genetic component because when one member of a set of identical twins develops GAD, the probability that the other twin will also get it is significantly increased.

Mechanisms

No one is completely sure what exactly leads to the development of GAD. However, there are certain factors that are believed to increase the risk of acquiring the condition. For example, metabolic and hormonal conditions like hyperthyroidism (overactivity of the thyroid gland), hyperadrenalism (too much adrenaline being released from the adrenal glands), and hypoglycemia (low blood sugar) are believed to stimulate a state of overactivity that may make a person feel anxious for no particular reason. Eating certain foods, such as chocolate and very sweet soft drinks, may also stimulate an individual's system and create a feeling of unease. These feelings may then become associated with events or circumstances that would not normally be worrisome but now become connected to the sensation of being physically aroused.

There are also psychological factors that may predispose someone toward GAD. One of these is a history of emotional, physical, or sexual abuse. Being involved in relationships that are unstable, like with someone who is an alcoholic or a drug abuser, is also associated with developing GAD.

Brain imaging studies have shown that people with GAD show increased activation in many parts of the brain compared to people who do not suffer from GAD. Finally, as mentioned earlier, GAD is often a feature of other types of psychiatric illnesses.

Treatment

Traditionally, benzodiazepines and tricyclic antidepressants (TCAs) have been the most prescribed drug treatments for GAD. However, selective serotonin reuptake inhibitors (SSRIs), as well as selective serotonin and norepinephrine reuptake inhibitors (SNRIs; for example, venlafaxine) and buspirone have also proven to be effective.

Benzodiazepines

Benzodiazepines have been shown to be very effective in the treatment of GAD. Chlordiazepoxide, lorazepam, diazepam, clonazepam, and alprazolam are the most commonly prescribed benzodiazepines for this condition (Figure 1.5). A number of people who are given these drugs for GAD will have difficulty stopping them. This is because withdrawal symptoms and returning feelings of anxiety (often called "rebound anxiety") are very common when benzodiazepine use is discontinued. Because of this, doctors often use long-acting benzodiazepines such as clonazepam that are gradually metabolized in the body rather than short-acting benzodiazepines like alprazolam. Another way of lessening the impact of removing benzodiazepines is to prescribe an SSRI to be taken during the period of withdrawal from the benzodiazepine drug. For example, studies have shown that taking imipramine improves withdrawal symptoms. Short-term cognitive-behavioral therapy throughout the period of benzodiazepine withdrawal also helps reduce the severity of symptoms.

Patients with drug or alcohol problems and those with chronic pain disorders or severe personality disorders almost certainly should not take benzodiazepines because of the high potential for developing benzodiazepine dependence.

Antidepressants

Venlafaxine, paroxetine, sertraline, imipramine, and trazodone have all proven effective in relieving symptoms of GAD. Venlafaxine, a combined serotonin and norepinephrine reuptake blocker, may be an exceptionally good choice for people who have other psychiatric illnesses in addition to GAD, or when it is not clear whether the patient has GAD or a depressive illness, or both. Although, to date, only certain SSRIs have been

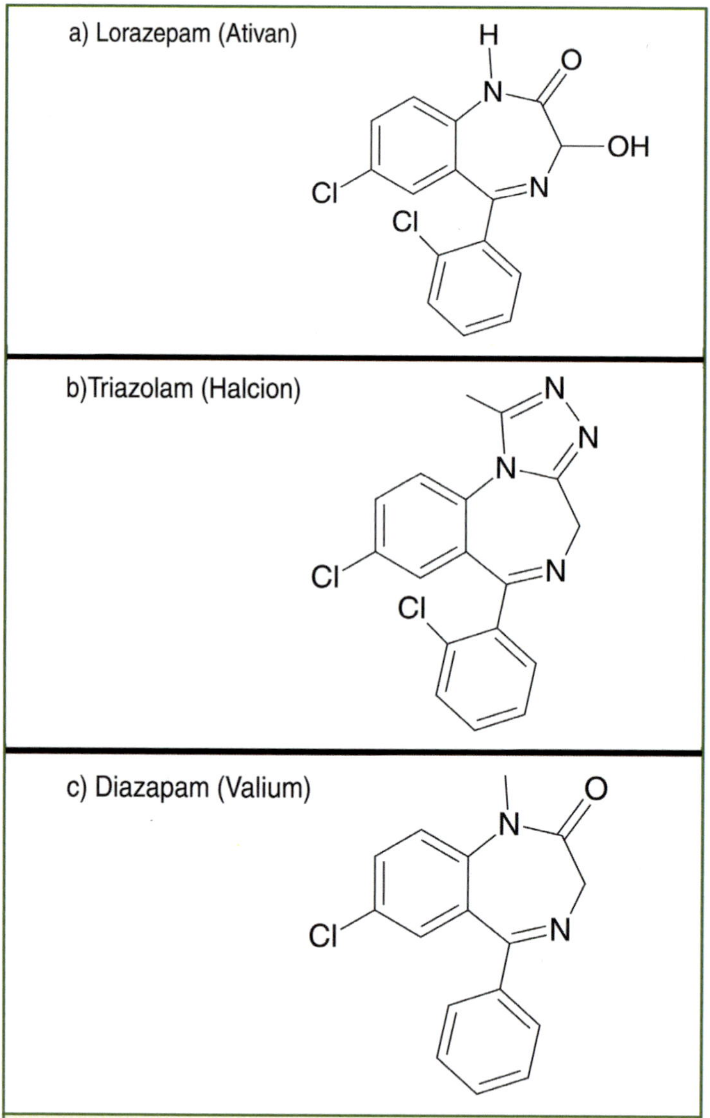

Figure 1.5 (A) Lorazepam (Ativan), (B) Trialzolam (Halcion), and (C) Diazapam (Valium) are the most common medications prescribed to patients with general anxiety disorder (GAD). These anti-anxiety drugs are quickly metabolized, and thus can cause withdrawal symptoms and rebound anxiety when discontinued.

approved by the U.S. Food and Drug Administration (FDA) for the treatment of GAD, most SSRIs are probably similarly effective in treating the symptoms of GAD. Therefore, the choice of which SSRI to administer can be based upon side effects and cost. In children and adolescents with GAD, one study found that the SSRI sertraline was a safe and effective treatment, with positive results apparent within four weeks of starting the drug.

SSRIs or SNRIs may produce side effects that include restlessness and insomnia, symptoms that may be similar to the symptoms of GAD and may cause patients to stop taking their medication. Starting at a lower dose and gradually working up to a full dose as the patient becomes better able to tolerate the drug minimizes these side effects.

Buspirone

Buspirone has been shown to be as effective as benzodiazepines for the treatment of GAD. However, it appears to take several weeks for this drug to be effective. The big advantage of using buspirone instead of benzodiazepines is that buspirone does not have the sedative effect, physical dependence, and withdrawal symptoms often seen with benzodiazepines. Buspirone does, however, cause stomach upset in some patients that may discourage patients from taking the drug.

DRUG TREATMENT FOR ANXIETY

Although there appear to be many different types of anxiety illnesses, the pharmacological treatment for almost all of them consists of very similar drugs. This is probably because all of the drugs used for anxiety act generally on many brain systems, with the overall result being a reduction in anxiety. The development and the action of the major drugs used to treat anxiety disorders will be discussed in the following chapters. The challenge for the future will be to develop drugs that target the specific brain areas involved in each unique anxiety disorder.

THERAPY OR DRUGS
(Interview with Mark Ilgen, Ph.D.)

The following is an interview conducted with Mark Ilgen, a clinical psychologist who works at Stanford University in Palo Alto, California.

Q: Do drugs and therapy work to treat anxiety?

A: Based on evidence from numerous experimental studies, both psychotherapy and medications are effective treatments for anxiety disorders. Despite the general effectiveness of these treatments, each has its own set of advantages and disadvantages. I feel that treatment for anxiety disorders is most effective if the treatment provider and the patient honestly discuss the pros and cons of each treatment. That way, they can choose the one that is best for each individual. Additionally, even when treatment appears to be working well, it is worthwhile for the patient and treatment provider to periodically discuss the benefits and side effects of the treatment and the option of switching treatments.

Q: Which treatment is best?

A: In an ideal world, we would be able to identify the specific treatment that is best for each person. Then, treatment providers would be able to suggest the type of treatment that has the highest probability of success for each individual. Unfortunately, we are a long way off from knowing exactly which treatment is best for each person. Additionally, every person is different in terms of their preferences for treatment: Some people are opposed to taking medications; others see psychosocial treatments as overly time-consuming or disruptive in their lives. Often, patients have to take a "leap of faith" and try a treatment before they know for sure if it will work for them. The good news is that even if this strategy does not work, other strategies exist and can be tried if the first strategy is not very helpful.

Q: What do you mean when you say "therapy?"

A: The term therapy often means many different things to different people. In terms of therapy for anxiety disorders, cognitive-behavioral therapy (sometimes called simply "behavioral therapy") appears to be the most effective type of treatment. The exact components of cognitive-behavioral treatments change depending on the specific type of anxiety that is being treated, but all contain some exposure to the feared stimulus in combination with help in understanding the role that thoughts (or fears) play in maintaining the anxiety. These treatments have received solid support either on their own or in combination with other treatments, such as medication or support groups. In fact, some evidence exists that cognitive-behavioral therapy may be more effective on its own than in combination with medications. This is a controversial issue and undoubtedly will receive a good deal of attention from researchers in the near future. In the meantime, it is important for people to know that the best-understood treatments for anxiety are more than just "talk therapy;" they involve concrete tools and specific steps for managing symptoms and avoiding future problems. Sometimes, patients may opt for more in-depth therapy after they learn to better control their anxiety. For others, a few sessions of structured treatment are all that they need to feel better.

2

Review of the Nervous System

BRAIN AREAS AND NEUROTRANSMITTER SYSTEMS RELATED TO ANXIETY

Before we can understand how anti-anxiety drugs work to ease the symptoms of anxiety-based illnesses, we need at least a basic idea of how the brain produces fearful and anxious states. First, we must understand which parts of the brain control particular aspects of the expression of fear and anxiety, and how these brain areas interact with each other to cause a certain type of behavior. The first step involves learning which anatomical structures within the brain control emotion expression. The second step is to understand how these structures communicate with one another.

Consider a circumstance in which you suddenly become very frightened. Imagine, for instance, that you are hiking through a forest and, just as you go around a corner in the trail, a mountain lion jumps out of the trees a few feet in front of you. Even before you can say "mountain lion" to yourself, your heart has begun to pound in your chest, your blood pressure rises, the pupils in your eyes dilate, your breathing becomes rapid, and your facial expression changes. Part of your brain has ordered the release of powerful substances called "stress hormones" into your bloodstream. These work to deliver more energy to your muscles. You find that your movement has completely stopped, and that you are almost frozen to the spot where you stand. In addition, your senses seem to be magnified. Somewhere in the forest, a twig snaps and the sound startles you much more than it would have just moments before. You are vividly aware of everything in your immediate surroundings. Suddenly, you realize that you may be able to escape through an alternate trail off to your right. You are almost painfully conscious of feeling very afraid.

These responses are the familiar reactions we all experience when we are confronted with a frightening situation. They involve the activation of many brain areas (Figure 2.1). A region at the base of the brain, just above the brain stem, called the **hypothalamus**, controls changes in blood pressure, pupil dilation, heart rate, and the release of stress hormones into the bloodstream. A region deep in the brain called the **central gray** suppresses motor activation and causes "freezing behavior." Another brain stem region called the **recticular net** heightens the reflex response to a sudden loud noise that results in an increased startle reaction. Other areas within the brain stem, called the nucleus of the solitary track and the locus ceruleus, release a specific neurotransmitter, **norepinephrine** (also called **noradrenaline**), which controls emotional arousal and increases attention. In addition, parts of the **cerebral cortex**, the "thinking" areas of the brain, cause the conscious feeling of being afraid.

As is very apparent, fear elicits many changes, both physical and emotional, that are controlled by different parts of the brain (Figure 2.2). Thus, the question becomes, is there one area or region of the brain that acts to synchronize all the different aspects of being afraid or anxious? Over the last 75 years, a considerable amount of evidence has determined that the brain regions responsible for coordinating the response to fear and anxiety are two relatively small areas, one on each side of the brain in the lower sections of both the right and left temporal lobe. Because the anatomists who first characterized these regions thought that they resembled the shape of almonds, they named these areas the *amygdala*, the Greek word for "almond."

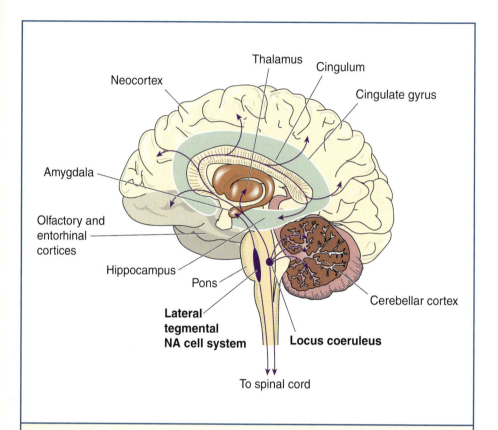

Figure 2.1 Fear responses involve the activation of many brain areas. The hypothalamus controls physical changes in the body, such as increased blood pressure and dilated pupils. The central gray area causes freezing behavior, the reticular net triggers a reflex response, and norepinephrine increases attention.

What evidence led medical researchers to conclude that the amygdala mediates the response to fear and anxiety? The first indication of the amygdala's importance in emotional reactivity was obtained in the 1930s by two scientists at the University of Chicago, Hienrich Kluver and Paul Bucy. They noted drastic changes in the behavior of rhesus monkeys after bilateral (on both sides of the brain) removal of the temporal lobe. One of the most striking behavioral changes

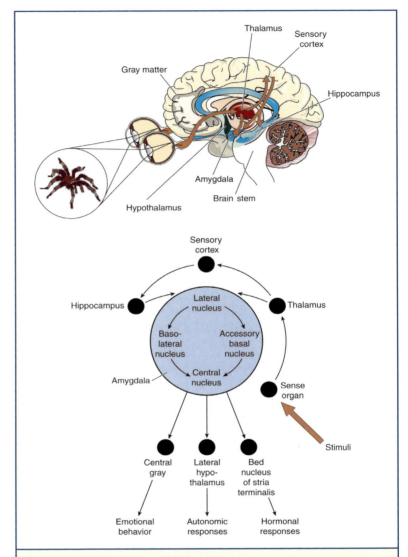

Figure 2.2 Fear elicits both physical and emotional changes that are coordinated by the amygdala. When a person sees a fear-inducing stimulus (the spider), the image reaches the thalamus, which is relayed to the cortex and hippocampus and projected to the lateral nucleus of the amygdala. Once the information reaches the amygdala's central nucleus, the thalamus, hippocampus, and cortex each produce a different fear response.

in these monkeys was the absence of fear. Usually, monkeys avoid humans and run if they are approached by people or other animals. However, the monkeys in the Kluver-Bucy experiments were exceedingly tame and even allowed their human caretakers to stroke them. There were changes in how much the monkeys vocalized and in their facial expressions when they encountered fear-engendering stimuli. These reactions, like the unusual tameness, indicated that a reduction in fear or anxiety had resulted from the surgery. It is true, of course, that the monkeys in this experiment had had a lot more brain tissue than just the amygdala removed. However, many later experiments showed that the amygdala was indeed the area responsible for controlling fear and anxiety responses in the brain.

Even though the amygdala represents the hub of the fear and anxiety circuit in the brain, it does not act alone. The amygdala sends connections by way of **axons** to many other parts of the brain that are believed to control the different aspects or characteristics of fear and anxiety. These brain regions then send their own axons to many other parts of the brain that also play a role in generating emotional responses. For example, the amygdala sends axons to a part of the brain called the hippocampus. The hippocampus, whose name means "seahorse," was named because the scientists who first located it thought it looked like one of those ocean creatures. It is responsible for the formation of **declarative memory**. Declarative memories are the kind of memories that we can tell other people about. For example, telling someone what you did last Saturday is recalling a declarative memory. People who have damage to their hippocampi (the plural of *hippocampus*) have difficulty forming new memories. People who have severe damage to their hippocampi cannot remember any new facts or things that they have done for longer than a few minutes. For example, Leonard Shelby (played by Guy Pearce) suffered from short-term memory in the 2000 movie *Memento*.

The amygdala sends axons to the hippocampus and these inputs are believed to enhance the memory that the hippocampus makes of highly charged emotional events. This is why, for example, everyone remembers where they were and what they were doing on September 11, 2001, when the Twin Towers of the World Trade Center were destroyed, or, if they are old enough to remember when President John F. Kennedy was assassinated.

A different part of the brain that receives axons from the amygdala is an area called the bed nucleus of the stria terminalis. Scientists call it the BNST for short. This brain area is involved in long-lasting responses to things. For instance, when rats are in an environment that makes them uncomfortable, like a brightly lit area, they become very anxious. Rats do not like bright light. The BNST is believed to control this anxiety state. The BNST itself sends axons to many parts of the brain and modulates the activity of those regions.

Another part of the brain that receives a great deal of input from the amygdala is a region called the septum. The septum is important for the expression of aggression. Input to the septum from the amygdala changes the way the septum responds to threatening situations. One area of investigation in modern neuroscience is the interplay between the amygdala and the septum and how that controls aggressive behavior. One interesting hypothesis being researched is the idea that the less afraid a person or an animal is (that is, the less input that is coming from the amygdala), the more aggressive the person or animal becomes.

WHAT MIGHT GO WRONG

Although the brain areas described above help give us a sense of fear that allows us to escape dangerous situations, sometimes activation of these brain areas goes awry. When this happens, it often causes an anxiety-related disorder. Although no one is certain what the exact cause of anxiety illness is, studies from both human populations and experimental animals have suggested many possible factors. One of the most predominant factors is stress. When scientists use the word *stress*, they are referring to anything that causes a change from being able to maintain the normal best functioning state. The

HOW NEURONS WORK

Neurons are the specialized cells through which virtually all the processes that occur in the central nervous system take place, from the control of movement and autonomic functions like breathing to complicated tasks like producing conscious thoughts. Internally, neurons use a combination of chemical and electrical signals, while communication between neurons is done mainly through chemical messengers called neurotransmitters.

To understand how neurons communicate, the first place to start is the connection point between two neurons, which is a small, fluid-filled space called a synapse. At the synapse, the end or terminal part of one neuron (called an axon) sits right across from the branches (called dendrites) or cell body (called the soma) of another neuron. The neuron that sends the axon to the synapse is called the *presynaptic neuron* because it is the one releasing the chemical signal or neurotransmitter that will travel to the soma or dendrites of the *postsynaptic neuron* which will receive and respond to that signal. When a neurotransmitter crosses a synapse, it binds with receptors on the membrane of the post-synaptic neuron. This binding of neurotransmitter causes special channels to open up in the membrane, allowing ions (elements that have a charge when they are in water) that are positively charged to enter the postsynaptic neuron. Neuron membranes are made up of fat molecules that usually do not let ions pass through. Normally, the inside of a neuronal membrane has more negative ions than positive normal best functioning state is when the organism and all its systems are working at their best. This means that the body's metabolism is getting enough energy from food, the immune system is primed to deal with invading germs, the cardio-vascular system is ready if it is called on to supply blood for

ions and so is said to have a net negative charge inside relative to its outer side. When binding of a neurotransmitter causes channels in the membrane to let positive ions inside, the neuron becomes *depolarized,* or loses its negative charge relative to the outside of the membrane. If enough neuro-transmitter binds and enough positive ions enter the neuron, then more ion channels will open all along the axon of the postsynaptic neuron. This movement of positive charge down the axon is called an action potential. When the action potential reaches the end of the axon, the rush of positive charge causes the release of neurotransmitter. Thus, the postsynaptic neuron then becomes a presynaptic neuron, releasing its neurotransmitter across synapses to interact with other postsynaptic neurons.

Some neurons release neurotransmitters that cause the postsynaptic neuron to become more negatively charged on the inside, a situation called *hyperpolarization.* This reduces the chance that an action potential will occur. Neurotrans-mitters that depolarize a postsynaptic neuron are called excitatory and those that cause hyperpolariztion are called inhibitory. Sometimes the same neurotransmitter can excite some neurons and inhibit others. This happens because one kind of neurotransmitter can have several types of receptors. Some of these receptors will depolarize the postsynaptic neuron and some will hyperpolarize it. The effect of a partic-ular neurotransmitter, therefore, depends on what types of receptors are waiting for it on the postsynaptic neuron.

increased muscle use, the brain is able to analyze and respond to its environment. This state of affairs is often called "homeostasis." Usually, everyday occurrences do not severely disturb homeostasis. However, being chased by a predator, being injured in a fight, getting infected by a germ, or simply being very anxious about an important test can push homeostasis off-balance. This is what scientists mean when they use the word *stress*. The body has systems that act to restore homeostasis when this happens, but when stress is prolonged or happens over and over again, the body has trouble getting back to a normal state and illness can result. One of these illnesses is anxiety disorder.

Another factor that appears to predispose some people toward an anxiety illness is having a certain genetic makeup. Anxiety disorders often occur in people who are related. The most compelling evidence of this comes from a type of study called "twin studies." In these research studies, the percentage of identical twins where both suffer from an illness is compared to the percentage of nonidentical twins or other close relatives where both people have the illness. This is then compared to how often the illness occurs in an unrelated population. If the occurrence in twins is higher than the occurrence in nonidentical siblings and the occurrence in nonidentical siblings is higher than in an unrelated population, then there is probably a genetic influence in the development of the disease. Overall, studies of this sort have demonstrated that having a family history or a relative with an anxiety disorder makes it more likely that an individual will develop anxiety, too.

There is also evidence indicating that early life environment can have a big impact on the incidence of anxiety in adulthood. People who have experienced childhood trauma, particularly physical or sexual abuse or the loss of a caretaker, show an increased rate of anxiety disorders. Studies in rats and monkeys have shown that having a lack of maternal care during a crucial period of development produces an increased response to stressful situations when the animals reach adulthood. These studies suggest that early life trauma causes permanent changes that make an individual vulnerable to anxiety as an adult.

Finally, there is accumulating evidence that sex hormones can influence the development of an anxiety disorder. Sex hormones are those chemicals produced by the testes in males and the ovaries in females. The testes mainly produce the male sex hormone testosterone and the ovaries mostly produce the female sex hormones estrogen and testosterone. Sex hormones are believed to play a role in governing anxiety because roughly two to three times more women than men suffer from anxiety disorders. In women, the incidence of anxiety disorder is most common at times when the female sex hormones are increasing or decreasing, such as right before a woman has her menstrual period or right after she gives birth. There is also an increase in anxiety illness when a woman goes through menopause and experiences rapidly rising and falling sex hormone levels. Interestingly, estrogen given at a steady level reduces anxiety in both people and in animals, and testosterone has been shown to reduce anxiety both in male rats and in men who have low natural levels of the hormone. Therefore, it seems likely that either female sex hormones or simply having sex hormone levels that fluctuate may make one susceptible to anxiety illnesses.

3

Animal Models of Anxiety Disorders

In developing an animal model of diseases and disorders, scientists try to mimic some aspect of the disorder. This usually means that some signs or symptoms of the psychiatric disorder are expressed by the experimental animal used in the model. For example, in modeling fear, one might look for a specific trait that represents fear in the animal that is being used: For a rat, freezing behavior (that is, a complete cessation of movement) is the classical expression of fear. Researchers hope that by experimentally causing anxiety or fear in animals, they can create some of the brain changes that produce anxiety. Then it may be possible to test possible anti-anxiety drugs to see if they are useful. In this chapter, we will discuss some of the most widely used tests that are thought to reproduce anxiety-like states in animals, and look at the effectiveness of certain drugs that are used to treat anxiety in people.

CONFLICT TESTS

One of the most popular tests used to measure anxiety in animals are **operant conflict tests**. The word *operant* means that the subject, whether animal or human, must perform some task to bring about a specific result. In this kind of test, something that the animal likes or needs (such as food or water) is used as positive reinforcement to teach the animal to perform a task. For example, a rat might learn that pressing a lever brings the delivery of a food pellet. In this case, pressing the lever is the "operant" behavior and the food pellet is the "reinforcer" or "reward" that helps the rat learn that pressing the lever brings a food pellet. After the rat has learned this, a conflict is introduced. Usually, this conflict involves some kind of punishment that becomes associated with getting the reinforcer or reward. In the case described above, once the rat has learned that pressing the lever gets it a food pellet, then the pressing of the lever will also be paired with a mild foot shock. Now, for the rat to get the food, it also has to endure getting its feet shocked (an uncomfortable but not painful experience). This conflict causes anxiety in the rat. The more anxious the rat is, the less it will try to get the reward. To increase the desire for the reward, rats are often restricted in the food or water they get during the course of the experiment.

This kind of test has proven to have some merit for identifying drugs that reduce anxiety. Most benzodiazepines that have been tested produce an increase in the punished behavior (the rat still presses the lever in spite of getting shocked). However, amphetamines, a class of drugs that simply increase physical activity also increase punished behavior, and many drugs that are thought to reduce anxiety, such as morphine and SSRIs do not increase punished behavior. Researchers believe that these tests are really only good for identifying certain types of anti-anxiety drugs.

THE ELEVATED PLUS MAZE

The elevated plus maze measures how rats and mice react in an apparatus that has two distinct environments, one a brightly lit and exposed runway and the other a dark and walled runway. The two runways intersect in the center (giving the maze the appearance of a plus sign) and are about 30 inches (76 cm) off the ground. Because rodents are nocturnal (active at night) animals and dislike open and well-lit places, the elevated plus maze is said to be a natural, or ethologically-based, test of anxiety. When a rat or mouse is placed in the elevated plus maze, it is free to go wherever it likes. This kind of "approach/avoidance" behavior is considered an excellent measure of the amount of stress, anxiety, or fear the animal is experiencing. The elevated plus maze is probably the most commonly used test for measuring emotionality in rats and mice (Figure 3.1).

Several drugs have been shown to increase open arm exploration in the elevated plus maze. Both benzodiazepines and SSRIs consistently produce increased open arm time. States that increase anxiety in human beings, like alcohol withdrawal, result in decreased open arm exploration in rats, thus verifying that this is a good test of anxiety for rodents. In addition, procedures that produce states of anxiety in rats, like mild foot shock, forced swimming, social isolation, and exposure to novel environments also subsequently decrease open arm time, again indicating that this is an accurate test for anxiety in these animals (Figure 3.2).

THE DEFENSIVE BURYING TEST

Most animals have a natural defensive reaction to aversive objects in their environments. Rodents will avoid the aversive object and also bury the object beneath the bedding material in their cage. The defensive burying test takes advantage of this natural response and uses both the avoidance and the burying behaviors to determine the rodents' level of anxiety. The best-known procedure for this utilizes a metal rod that delivers a mild electric shock when touched. The amount of time the animal spends burying the rod, the height of the bedding pile used for burying, and the amount of time spent avoiding the area are all measured as levels of anxiety.

It is thought that this test for anxiety most closely resembles the behavior that accompanies a specific phobia. Because this burying behavior is consistent and does not decrease over time, it is also believed that this type of behavior resembles what is seen with obsessive-compulsive disorder. Benzodiazepines are an example of a drug that reduces both the avoidant and the burying behaviors in this test.

Figure 3.1 The elevated plus maze is a test to monitor stress, anxiety, and fear in rats and mice by measuring how they react when placed in an apparatus that has two distinct environments. The animal can choose to enter an unfamiliar area that is either brightly lit or dark. The approach/avoidance behavior displayed indicates whether the animal is under stress.

THE SOCIAL INTERACTION TEST

Rats are usually social animals. When two rats that are unfamiliar with each other are introduced, they will spend the first few minutes sniffing and touching one another. However, when rats are in an unfamiliar environment or when there is something about the environment that makes rats uncomfortable, like bright lights or a wide open space, they will spend much less time investigating a new acquaintance. Therefore, the amount of time that two rats spend interacting with each other in a new or uncomfortable (for the rat) environment

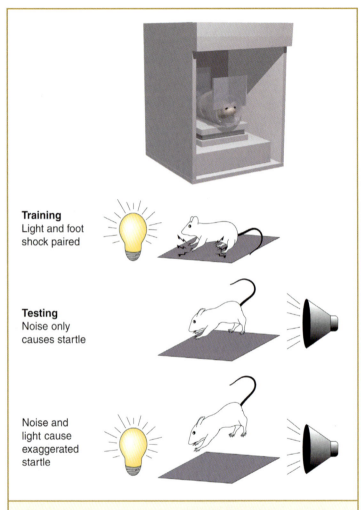

Figure 3.2 Procedures such as introducing light shock, noises, and a combination of the two are added to the elevated plus maze to determine anxiety levels of mice and rats.

can be used as a measure of anxiety. This kind of experiment is called the social interaction test. It has been shown to be very sensitive to many drugs that are believed to reduce anxiety. Benzodiazepines and barbiturates in particular increase social interaction between rats. Interestingly, SSRIs have no effect.

This test is also very sensitive to treatments that increase anxiety, such as injections of peptides like corticotropin-releasing factor, which is known to cause the release of stress hormones and produce anxiety.

THE ACOUSTIC STARTLE RESPONSE

Jumping in response to a sudden loud noise is a reflex called the acoustic startle response. Virtually all vertebrate animals (animals with a backbone) show this response. The size of the startle response increases when the animal or person is in a frightened or anxious state. You have likely experienced this yourself. It is easy to imagine that if you were walking down a dark city street in a dangerous part of town and heard a car backfire, you would jump much higher than if you were seated comfortably in your living room watching television and heard the same noise. Measuring the acoustic startle response is a reliable way to gauge the amount of fear or anxiety that an animal is experiencing.

Studies using the acoustic startle reflex have shown that the response decreases after the administration of benzodiazepines, while SSRIs have no effect. The acoustic startle response can be increased in rats simply by putting them in a brightly lit chamber. The acoustic startle response can also be increased in rats through a procedure called "fear-conditioning." In this test, rats are taught to connect the appearance of a light with receiving a mild shock on their feet. Once the rats have learned this association, they are tested for their startle response with the light on and with the light off. Because they think they will be shocked when the light is on, they jump higher when the acoustic noise occurs than they do when the noise is presented with the light off. This is called "fear-potentiated startle" and is a very good measure of how afraid the rat is. Once the rat has been trained in fear-potentiated startle, different drugs can be given and their effect on the startle response can be measured.

THE DEFENSIVE WITHDRAWAL TEST

Rodents do not like to be out in the middle of a large open space. This makes sense, because going into open spaces increases the likelihood that the rodent will be spotted by a predator. Scientists can use the natural desire rodents have to avoid open spaces as a measure of how anxious a rat or a mouse is. In the defensive withdrawal test, rats or mice are placed in a bright open space that has an enclosed dark box off to one side. The amount of time that the rodent spends inside the box compared with the amount of time the rodent spends outside is thought to be a measure of anxiety. This test has been shown to be fairly sensitive to drugs.

ARE MODELS OF ANXIETY CRUEL TO ANIMALS?

Many people worry that tests for anxiety using animals are harmful or cruel to the animals tested. Scientists also worry about this. No one enjoys inflicting discomfort or pain on a living creature. On the other hand, it is difficult to measure something aversive without somehow creating an aversive environment. Scientists try to come up with models that will reproduce the effect they want (in this case, anxiety) with the least amount of disturbance to the animal. In fact, in order to use animals for any scientific experiment, it is necessary to formally apply for permission to a panel of veterinarians and other animal care specialists. This panel reviews the proposed experiment and considers whether it is acceptable. Many times, the panel will insist that an experiment be changed if it causes too much pain or trauma to the animal. In this way, scientists and animal health experts hope to limit the amount discomfort to which any laboratory animal is subjected.

LEARNED HELPLESSNESS

Psychologists working at the University of Pennsylvania in the 1960s noticed that animals exposed to brief, inescapable shocks had great difficulty in their subsequent ability to learn that they could escape from the shocks they were receiving. Animals that were exposed to exactly the same amount of shock, but had control over it—that is, they could get away from it—were not impaired. It was as if the rats that had first experienced the inescapable shocks learned that it was useless to even try to escape so they simply behaved as if they were helpless to do anything about their situation. These experiments, later called "learned helplessness," offered evidence that a factor such as uncontrollability could hinder an animal's capacity to respond even when control was possible. Animals exposed to the inescapable stress showed a number of other symptoms such as sleep and eating disturbances, ulcers, and decreases in immune status. Because it appeared as if the animals had given up, learned helplessness was endorsed as an animal model for depression in humans, the justification being that exposure to uncontrollable and stressful life events leads to a feeling of loss of control, which ultimately leads to depressive behavior.

4

Benzodiazepines

The most common type of treatment physicians use to treat anxiety disorders consists of a class of drugs called the benzodiazepines. These drugs interact with a specific type of receptor in the brain called the $GABA_A$ receptor.

GABA is shorthand for γ(gamma)-aminobutyric acid. GABA is one of the most abundant neurotransmitters in the brain. Because GABA acts to reduce the activity or firing rate of neurons, it is called an inhibitory neurotransmitter. GABA accomplishes this inhibition through two types of receptors, both of which reduce the ability of neurons to fire an action potential. One of the receptors through which GABA works is a membrane receptor called the $GABA_B$ receptor. When GABA binds to this receptor, it produces a series of chemical signals inside the neuron that ultimately stops the neuron from activating. The second type of receptor, the one with which benzodiazepines interact, is called the $GABA_A$ receptor. Activation of the $GABA_A$ receptor causes a channel in the cell membrane of neurons to open and allow negative chloride ions to enter. The entry of these negative chloride ions reduces the excitability of the neuron and decreases that neuron's ability to fire an action potential. GABA opens this channel membrane by binding at a specific place on the $GABA_A$ receptor and changing the shape of the proteins that make up the receptor complex. It is this change in receptor shape that pulls open the ion channel. The location on the receptor that binds GABA is called the GABA binding site.

The $GABA_A$ receptor also has binding sites for many other substances besides GABA (Figure 4.1). All of these different binding

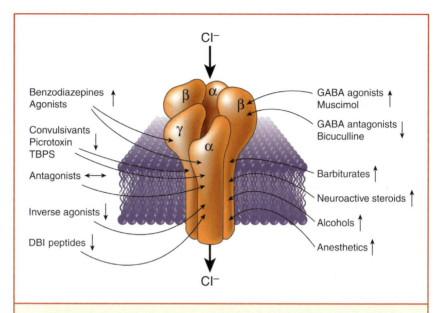

Cl⁻

Benzodiazepines
Agonists ↑

β α
β

GABA agonists ↑
Muscimol

γ

α

Convulsivants
Picrotoxin ↓
TBPS

Antagonists ↔

Inverse agonists ↓

DBI peptides ↓

GABA antagonists ↓
Bicuculline

Barbiturates ↑

Neuroactive steroids ↑

Alcohols ↑

Anesthetics ↑

Cl⁻

Figure 4.1 Benzodiazepines interact with the GABA_A receptor in the brain and activate the cell membrane of neurons to open and allow negative chloride ions (Cl⁻) to enter the neuron (α, β, γ subunits form the C1- ion). This entry inhibits that neuron's ability to fire an action potential. The GABA_A receptor also has binding sites for other substances, such as steroids, barbiturates, and alcohol.

sites bind molecules that modify the effect GABA has on the membrane channel. Some of these sites bind substances that enhance the effect of GABA and increase channel opening, while others reduce the effect of GABA and lessen channel opening. For example, the GABA_A receptor has a binding site for a class of molecules called steroids. These are molecules that include sex hormones like testosterone and estrogen as well as the substances that they change into inside the body. Depending on the type, steroids either act positively (increasing channel opening) or negatively (decreasing channel opening). There are also binding sites on the GABA_A receptor for compounds such as barbiturates, drugs like picrotoxin that cause convulsions, and alcohol. In addition, there is a specific binding site on the GABA$_A$ receptor for the subject of this chapter: benzodiazepines.

Before the 1950s, almost all drugs that reduced anxiety also had many other, mostly unwanted, effects. The most commonly prescribed anti-anxiety drugs were the barbiturates. Although they reduce anxiety, barbiturates also inhibit muscle activity and can produce lung congestion and heart failure. Barbiturates are highly physically and emotionally addictive and many people developed a severe physical dependency on them, even after relatively short-term use. Because of these concerns, scientists were eager to find a drug that would reduce anxiety without producing these negative side effects.

The first of the benzodiazepines was discovered by chemists working for the Swiss company Hoffman-LaRoche Pharmaceuticals who noticed that a compound accidentally made from a dye had a "taming" effect on rats. When they analyzed this compound, they found that it was made up of two ring-like structures: one made up of hydrogen and carbon atoms arranged in a six-ringed structure called a benzene ring, and the other a seven-ringed carbon and hydrogen structure containing two nitrogen atoms called a diazepine. The combination of these rings formed a compound that "fit" like a key into one part of the GABA$_A$ receptor and helped open the chloride channel when a molecule of GABA was simultaneously bound to its own binding site on the receptor. One way to picture this is to imagine that when GABA binds to the receptor, it acts like a hand pulling open the chloride channel. When both GABA and a benzodiazepine are bound to the receptor, another hand pulls on the first hand to help open the ion channel. It is important to remember, however, that the second hand (the benzodiazepine) only helps when the first hand (GABA) is already working to pull the channel open. It does not open the channel on its own.

To date, many different kinds of benzodiazepines have been produced (see Table 4.1). In the 1950s, chlordiazepoxide

Table 4.1 Benzodiazepines

GENERIC NAME	BRAND NAME*
Alprazolam	Kalma, Xanax
Bromazepam	Lexotan
Clobazam	Frisium
Clonazepam	Klonopin
Diazepam	Antenex , Ducene ,Valium
Flunitrazepam	Hypnodorm, Rohypnol
Lorazepam	Ativan
Nitrazepam	Alodorm, Mogadon
Oxazepam	Alepam, Murelax, Serepax
Temazepam	Euhypnos, Nocturne, Normison, Temaze, Temtabs
Triazolam	Halcion

* Benzodiazepines are manufactured by several different drug companies and often have different brand names.

NAME*	APPROXIMATE DURATION OF DRUG ACTION**
SHORT	
Triazolam	2 Hours
Oxazepam	8 Hours
Temazepam	10 Hours
MEDIUM	
Bromazepam	12 Hours
Lorazepam	12 Hours
Alprazolam	14 Hours
LONG	
Clobazam	18 Hours
Flunitrazepam	25 Hours
Nitrazepam	28 Hours
Clonazepam	30 Hours
Diazepam	32 Hours

* Benzodiazepines are classified as short, medium, and long acting. This relates to the duration of drug action in the body.

** Length of action can also be influenced by the health of the patient's liver and the patient's age and weight.

(librium) was researched as the first benzodiazepine agent. It was introduced in 1960, and was followed by diazepam (Valium) in 1963. Diazepam was much more potent than its predecessor and seemed to be better at treating many different types of anxiety. Since these agents were introduced, many other benzodiazepines have been developed and used to treat anxiety. These drugs are still widely used today.

All benzodiazepines have basically the same structure and work in relatively the same way by interacting with the $GABA_A$ receptor. They differ from one another in the way they are absorbed, metabolized, and excreted by the body. For example, lorazepam is a benzodiazepine that is absorbed slowly from the digestive system tract. It is often prescribed to prevent early morning wakefulness because it becomes active about five hours after it is taken. Thus, it begins to work at the time when the person suffering from this type of insomnia would be waking up and allows the person to continue sleeping.

HOW DO BENZODIAZEPINES WORK IN THE BRAIN?

Benzodiazepines act on the amygdala to reduce anxiety. However, benzodiazepines do not solely affect the output region of the amygdala that we have discussed previously (the central nucleus). Instead, these drugs affect the part of the amygdala where incoming sensory and cognitive information converge—the basolateral amygdala. It is this area of the amygdala that receives and controls the output of signals that tell the animal or human being that something scary or dangerous is occurring and should be heeded.

Benzodiazepines also act on two other brain regions that we have discussed in relation to anxiety. One of these areas is the lateral septum. The septum, as you will recall, is involved in the expression of aggressive behavior. Curiously, benzodiazepines infused into the lateral part of the septum decrease electric probe burying but do not interfere with avoidance of the probe, while injection of benzodiazepines into the central amygdala decrease the avoidance of the probe by the rat, but do not decrease burying of the probe. This implies that the septum is involved in "active" behaviors related to fear and anxiety, while the central amygdala is related to avoidance or "passive" behaviors.

The other brain region involved in benzodiazepine effects on anxiety is the central gray region. Benzodiazepines injected into the central gray have been shown to reduce anxiety in the elevated plus maze.

NEUROTRANSMITTER SYSTEMS THAT ARE AFFECTED BY BENZODIAZEPINES

We have already learned that benzodiazepines act on $GABA_A$ receptors to amplify the effect of GABA and cause increased negative or inhibitory currents to enter the neuron and thus decrease the chance of that neuron firing an action potential. Because an action potential causes the release of neuro-transmitter when it reaches the end of the neuron, the neurotransmitter that that particular neuron releases is reduced (Figure 4.2). In this section, we will look at the major neurotransmitter system that is affected when benzo-diazepines are administered.

There is a lot of evidence that the major neurotransmitter system affected by benzodiazepines is the one that controls the release of the neurotransmitter norepinephrine (also known as noradrenaline). Studies suggest that people with anxiety illnesses have increased release of norepinephrine and that this continued release causes a depletion of this neuro-transmitter and a shutdown of the neurons that are releasing it. This is important because norepinephrine is involved in making an animal or person focused or attentive to what is going on in the environment. When this neurotransmitter is overreleased, it causes anxiety. When no more norepinephrine is available for release, it causes a feeling of exhaustion.

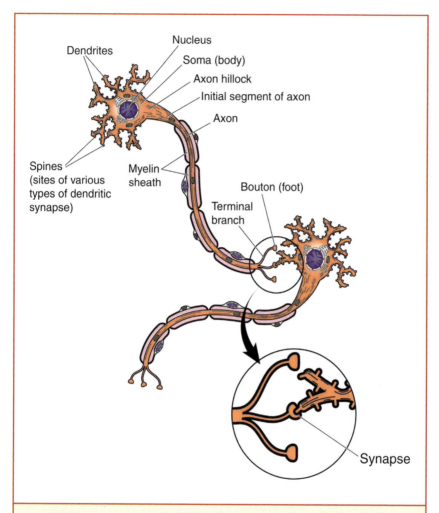

Figure 4.2 The brain has billions of cells called neurons. Each neuron, like the one shown here, has an axon that transmits information to other cells. The end of the axon, or the terminal branch, typically makes contact with the dendrites on other cells.

Norepinephrine is released into the brain by a few pathways that originate in the brain stem and one pathway in another part of the brain called the pons. The pathway in the pons, called the locus coeruleus, is particularly important because it is responsible for most of the release of norepinephrine in the parts of the brain that control fear and anxiety. Several studies have shown that treatment with benzodiazepines selectively decreases norepinephrine release in these areas, and also stops the expression of fear and anxiety-like behaviors. Interestingly, if the animals are given a drug that blocks the effect of benzodiazepines, then there is no effect on norepinephrine and anxiety behaviors increase.

THE MEDICINAL USE OF BENZODIAZEPINES
Because benzodiazepines have few side effects and do not usually cause indigestion or other types of gastrointestinal (digestive) upset, they are prescribed for several conditions. The most common use of benzodiazepines is, of course, to treat anxiety. Because most benzodiazepines are equally effective in treating most types of anxiety, which benzodiazepine is prescribed often depends on the preferences of the doctor. However, alprazolam and clonazepam are used most often to treat panic disorder. Diazepam, which was the most prescribed benzodiazepine in the 1970s and 1980s, was found to remain in the body for a very long time, leading to the possibility that an unhealthy amount of drug may build up. Today, alprazolam, which breaks down much faster in the body, is the most often prescribed benzodiazepine for the majority of anxiety disorders.

Benzodiazepines are also used for several other conditions that are related to, but not actually termed, anxiety. For example, benzodiazepines are commonly given as "soporific" or "hypnotic" drugs (drugs that help people sleep). One of the benzodiazepines, flurazepam, is the most frequently prescribed hypnotic drug in the United States. Benzodiazepines also are administered as muscle relaxants, and can even reduce the occurrence of seizures or convulsions. Another common use of benzodiazepines is in alcohol withdrawal. Someone who is trying to stop drinking alcohol is usually given a heavy dose of benzodiazepines that is slowly reduced over the first three to seven days of alcohol withdrawal. Taking benzodiazepines at the beginning of alcohol withdrawal helps reduce not only the anxiety that goes along with the cessation of drinking but also reduces the involuntary trembling (called delirium tremens) that often takes place when someone suddenly stops drinking large amounts of alcohol.

SIDE EFFECTS AND TOXICITY

Benzodiazepines have very few side effects. As you would expect, because benzodiazepines work by enhancing the inhibitory neurotransmitter GABA, the most common complaint from people who use benzodiazepines is that they feel drowsy, sedated, slowed down, or experience slurred speech. It is important to emphasize that people taking benzodiazepines should not drive or operate dangerous machinery until they have determined how the drug will affect them.

One side effect that concerns patients and physicians alike is memory loss, or amnesia. This usually happens only when benzodiazepines are given intravenously (through a needle in a vein). Some people report that they have difficulty learning new tasks when taking benzodiazepines. However, these effects usually last only a short time and go away after the person has taken the drug for a while.

Another factor that makes the benzodiazepines the anti-anxiety drug of choice for many people is the finding that benzodiazepines have little potential for abuse. Long-term use does not lead patients to take increased doses or try different drugs.

There are certain drugs that interact with the benzodiazepines and result in enhancement or a decrease in the effectiveness.

Buspirone is a useful drug because it produces a reduction in anxiety without having a sedative effect. Thus, it can be used instead of benzodiazepines when the sedative actions of the benzodiazepines are not appropriate. For example, someone who works with machinery would not want to be drowsy on the job.

Buspirone does not cause drowsiness because, unlike the benzodiazepines which act at the GABA receptor, it is believed that buspirone exerts its anti-anxiety effects by acting on one of the major receptors for serotonin, called the serotonin 1A receptor. When there are low levels of serotonin in the synapse between a serotonin-releasing neuron and its postsynaptic partner neuron, then buspirone appears to activate this receptor. However, when there is excess serotonin in the synapse, buspirone acts to inactivate or block this receptor .

Buspirone has been shown to be very effective in treating generalized anxiety disorder (GAD). It is especially useful when combined with a benzodiazepine, probably because using these two drugs together causes the activation of two neurotransmitter systems (GABA and serotonin).

Buspirone has very few side effects, which is another reason it is widely prescribed.

5

Antidepressants: (MAOIs and Tricyclics)

Because of the strong side effects and risk of dependency associated with benzodiazepines, antidepressants are often the first line of pharmacological treatment for anxiety disorders. There are three general classes of antidepressants: monamine oxidase inhibitors (MAOIs), tricyclic antidepressants (TCAs), and selective serotonin reuptake inhibitors (SSRIs). MAOIs and TCAs were the first anti-depressants used to treat depression and anxiety disorders, and because of their action on catecholamine neurotransmitters like norepinephrine, it was believed that deficits in the functioning of these systems were responsible for lowered mood and anxiety (Figure 5.1). (Catecholamines are a class of neurotransmitter made from the amino acid tyrosine; they are structurally very similar.) However, it was soon discovered that these drugs also affected serotonin systems, and recent research has focused more on serotonin mechanisms in depression and anxiety. Serotonin systems seem to play a role in many different behaviors, since serotonin is found throughout the brain. The advent of the SSRIs promoted the idea of a serotonin basis for depression and anxiety, particularly because the SSRIs have less serious side effects than the other classes of antidepressants, because they target fewer systems.

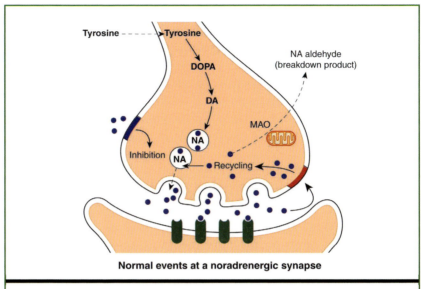

Normal events at a noradrenergic synapse

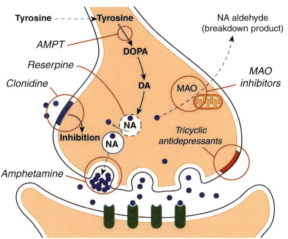

Drug effects at a noradrenergic synapse

Figure 5.1 Diagram of a noradrenergic (NA) synapse. After an NA neurotransmitter is recycled back into a neuron, the MAO enzyme breaks it down. MAOIs block the MAO enzyme, causing a buildup of NA transmitters inside the neuron, so that more are released into the synapse. Tricyclics block the recycling of the NA neurotransmitters back into the neuron.

It is likely that depression and anxiety disorders are associated with problems in several brain systems, and, indeed, different drugs appear to be effective in different people. Even though SSRIs are currently the first choice of drugs for treating many anxiety disorders, other classes of antidepressants are tried if the SSRIs prove ineffective.

NOREPINEPHRINE

Both norepinephrine and serotonin have been implicated in anxiety disorders and depression. Although scientists generally believe that MAOIs and TCAs are beneficial because they target serotonin systems, there is some evidence that specifically targeting the norepinephrine system can help some patients. Certain TCAs preferentially activate norepinephrine systems. These and other norepinephrine-selective drugs have been shown to help alleviate some cases of depression.

Norepinephrine is made in cells located in the brain stem, mostly in a group of cells called the locus coeruleus. These neurons send widespread projections throughout the brain. This distribution has functional consequences. Small disturbances in the locus coeruleus can have a large impact on many different brain areas at the same time, and thus influence many behaviors. Disorders of emotion and mood are similar in that they simultaneously impact many different behaviors. Therefore, it is reasonable to suggest that norepinephrine might affect emotion in some ways.

It is important to recognize that different parts of the brain regulate different behaviors. Drugs that raise levels of norepinephrine all over the brain are likely to influence many behaviors. The action of norepinephrine in each area might be very different, depending on what kind of receptor it binds. In the brain, norepinephrine can bind to four types of receptors: alpha 1, alpha 2, beta 1, and beta 2. Alpha 2 receptors cause inhibition and are considered autoreceptors because they are found on norepinephrine neurons, yet they inhibit the release of norepinephrine). Thus, these cells can regulate themselves because when they activate and release norepinephrine, they shut themselves off through a process called "feedback inhibition." The other three receptor subtypes increase the excitability of neurons.

The locus coeruleus tends to become active when an organism is presented with something that it must pay attention to, like a new object in the environment, and quiets down during periods when attention to the environment is minimal (like when we are sleeping). These cells may play a role in controlling arousal, focusing attention, and coordinating the responses to stimuli. The projections from the locus coeruleus to the frontal and prefrontal areas of the cortex may be particularly important in influencing mood. Activating this pathway can elevate the mood. Making changes in norepinephrine levels in other parts of the brain can also improve attention and concentration as well as memory problems associated with depression, schizophrenia, and Alzheimer's disease.

MONAMINE OXIDASE INHIBITORS (MAOIS)

In the early 1950s, the MAOI iproniazid was tried to treat tuberculosis. Researchers noticed that even when iproniazid was not effective in treating the tuberculosis, many of their patients seemed to be happier. Soon, iproniazid was put to use to treat depression. Later, MAOIs became the first antidepressants shown to be effective for the treatment of social anxiety disorder, and have since been used in the treatment of all of the anxiety disorders.

Iproniazid and other MOAIs act by inhibiting the action of the enzyme monoamine oxidase. This enzyme is found inside and outside of cells and helps break down several molecules, including the monoamine neurotransmitters norepinephrine, dopamine, and serotonin. The result of inhibiting this enzyme is that the levels of these neurotransmitters increase in the brain, which is thought to produce the therapeutic effects of these drugs.

Not long after their introduction, it was discovered that MAOIs could have serious and sometimes fatal interactions with other medications and foods that have high levels of tyramine. Tyramine is found in foods like cheese, wine, beer, liver, and even chocolate, and can increase blood pressure. MAOIs interact with certain medications and foods, raising blood pressure so much that fatal results can occur. To be used safely, these drugs must be taken with a restricted diet.

Two types of the MAO enzymes have been found. They are called MAO-A and MAO-B. MAO-A is found in norepinephrine and serotonin synapses, while MAO-B is found in dopamine synapses. Scientists believe that the therapeutic effects of MAOIs are a result of inhibiting MAO-A, while most of the side effects result from actions at MAO-B. The traditional, older MAOIs cannot select which MAO type they affect, so current studies are investigating drugs that might be more selective.

One important point is that the older MAOIs are irreversible. They act by binding with the MAO enzyme so tightly that the bond cannot be broken. The only way to regain MAO function is to produce new enzymes. This means that MAOIs work for a period of time even after the patient has stopped taking them. Therefore, the dietary restrictions must be maintained for a while after MAOI treatment has stopped.

New MAOI drugs are being developed that are both selective for MAO-B and reversible. The hope is that these drugs can be effective without causing the serious side effects associated with older MAOIs. Although research is promising, these new MAOIs have yet to be widely used in the treatment of anxiety disorders, possibly because of the overwhelming success of the SSRIs.

Since MAOIs have dangerous risks and since other, less obviously dangerous antidepressants exist, MAOIs are not often prescribed. However, when SSRIs fail, MAOIs may be used and are effective in many cases. Two of the older MAOI drugs still used to treat anxiety disorders are phenelzine, which is sold under the brand name Nardil, and tranylcypromine, which is sold under the brand name Parnate.

TRICYCLIC ANTIDEPRESSANTS

Shortly after iproniazid was shown to have antidepressant properties, imipramine was introduced as the first tricyclic antidepressant. These drugs received the name "tricyclic" because their structure contains three molecular rings. At first, imipramine was investigated as a possible treatment for the psychotic episodes associated with schizophrenia, a severe mental disorder that causes hallucinations and delusions, because it was chemically similar to another effective anti-schizophrenia drug. Imipramine did not reduce the severity of psychotic episodes, but it did elevate the mood of the patients who took it. In the late 1950s, it was released in the United States under the name Tofranil for the treatment of depression.

Since that time, many other tricyclic antidepressants have been studied and put into use. They are all structurally related to imipramine. The active metabolite of imipramine is desipramine. This means that imipramine breaks down into desipramine in the body, and the resulting desipramine actually improves mood. Because their structures are so similar, scientists assume that they have a similar action in the body.

In the 1950s, the drug reserpine was studied because it lowered blood pressure by affecting catecholamines like norepinephrine, epinephrine, and dopamine. Researchers found that the early antidepressants reversed the effects of reserpine. They reasoned that antidepressants increased catecholamines between nerve cells, and that this caused their antidepressant effects. This became known as the "catecholamine hypothesis." Catecholamines were studied extensively as mediators of depression.

Although there was some evidence for a catecholamine influence on depression, it became clear that this set of neurotransmitters was not the whole story. By the 1980s, attention shifted to the serotonin neurotransmitter system. Importantly, tricyclic antidepressants were found to modulate both serotonin systems and catecholamines. Increasingly, serotonin systems became the target for treatments of anxiety and depression, partly because of the effectiveness of drugs that selectively target serotonin in treating these disorders. In most cases, it has been assumed that the effectiveness of the tricyclic antidepressants was due to their action on serotonin systems. Currently, drugs that target the serotonin system are generally tried first in the treatment of anxiety disorders. If these drugs fail, then doctors will likely prescribe a TCA.

Like the MAOI drugs, TCAs act on many different neurotransmitter systems. Their therapeutic action is believed to occur by reducing the reuptake of serotonin and norepinephrine, thereby prolonging the action of these neurotransmitters. However, TCAs also affect histamine, acetylcholine, and dopamine systems in the brain, which can produce many side effects. For example, although histamine in the body is associated with inflammation and the response of the immune system, histamine in the brain is a neurotransmitter associated with arousal. TCAs block histamine receptors, producing drowsiness and lethargy (for the same reason, some antihistamines taken to combat allergies can get into the brain and cause drowsiness). Other side effects include breast enlargement, confusion, diarrhea, dry mouth, hallucinations, hives, high blood pressure, nausea, numbness, tremors, and vomiting. One other disadvantage of TCAs is that their therapeutic action can decrease over time.

SELECTIVE SEROTONIN REUPTAKE INHIBITORS

Currently, the most often prescribed class of drugs for the treatment of anxiety disorders is the SSRIs. Although several neurotransmitters have been linked to mood and affect, serotonin has received most of the interest in the last decade. This is partly due to the overwhelming commercial success of Prozac and other SSRIs in the treatment of depression and anxiety. These drugs target serotonin systems and appear to have a therapeutic benefit in many mental problems that are linked to emotion.

SEROTONIN: ANATOMY AND PHYSIOLOGY

Serotonin (sometimes abbreviated 5-HT) is a neurotransmitter made from the amino acid tryptophan (which is found

AUTORECEPTORS AND HOMEOSTASIS

The nervous system has several ways to maintain a stable and constant environment, called "homeostasis." Autoreceptors are a form of "feedback" inhibition, which help maintain homeostasis. When a neuron is excited, it can release neurotransmitters into the synapse that activate receptors on neighboring cells, communicating information through the nervous system. When a neurotransmitter is released, it also binds to receptors on the neuron that released it, which serves to inhibit further release. In this way, neurons can regulate their own release, so that they don't release too much neurotransmitters into the brain, which might overexcite or overinhibit neighboring neurons or deplete the neuron's own store of neurotransmitters.

It is thought that some problems with brain functioning might be due to breakdowns in this autoreceptor feedback system. Both norepinephrine and serotonin have autoreceptor feedback systems in the nuclei in which the cells originate. These systems appear to be affected in some models of anxiety.

in foods like turkey and milk). Whereas cells that make other neurotransmitters are often found all over the brain, serotonin is produced in a relatively small group of brain areas that are collectively called the raphe nuclei (Figure 5.2). These areas are found in "lower" parts of the brain (the brain stem) and represent a small number of cells when compared to the total number of neurons in the brain. Moreover, well over half of the brain's serotonergic cells are found in the dorsal and median raphe nuclei, and these two nuclei supply most of the serotonin to the "higher" (forebrain) structures that may be responsible for things like emotion.

Although serotonin is made in a relatively small number of neurons, these cells have many widespread projections. Barry Jacobs at Princeton University and Efrain Azmitia at New York University calculated in 1992 that although serotonergic cells make up approximately 1/1,000,000 of all neurons in a rat's brain, they account for as many as 1/500 of all axon terminals (projections) in the rat cortex (the layer of neurons found on the surface of the brain). These figures suggest that *each* serotonergic neuron sends, on average, 2,000 projections to the neurons on the surface of the brain! Thus, serotonin is anatomically much like norepinephrine, in that small changes in the serotonin nuclei can profoundly impact many different areas of the brain—and many different behaviors.

The effect of the release of any neurotransmitter depends on the type of receptor that it binds. One challenge in understanding serotonergic function in the brain is that at least 18 subtypes of serotonin receptors have so far been found, each with its own mechanism of action. Scientists have debated the reasons for this extreme number of types of receptor for one neurotransmitter (serotonin outnumbers most other neurotransmitters in this regard). It has been suggested that this diversity allows for more complicated signaling between brain cells that could not occur with just one or two receptor types. As a result, communication between cells is not simply

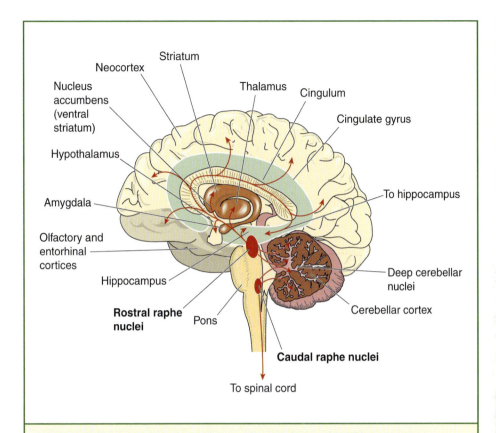

Figure 5.2 Serotonin is made in a small group of brain areas that are called the raphe nuclei. This view of the brain shows that the raphe nuclei form a continuous collection of cell groups throughout the brain stem. Serotonin is carried to other areas of the brain, such as the cortex, corpus striatum, and hippocampus.

excitation or inhibition, but rather a complicated mixture of both, along with some other, longer-lasting effects.

Given how complex serotonin can be, it is not surprising that the serotonergic system is still poorly understood and heavily debated by scientists. This debate is fueled by the increasing use of serotonergic drugs to treat emotional disorders, and an increasing need to understand how these drugs are working. Between 1985 and 1994, hospital visits in which an SSRI was prescribed rose from under one million per year to 11 million per year. In 1994, SSRI drug visits accounted for almost 20% of all visits involving drugs for *any* psychological problems. In 2004, SSRI use for the treatment of panic disorder alone cost $23 million, with $21 million of that paid for by tax money.

DEPRESSION AND ANXIETY

Traditionally, SSRIs have been used in the treatment of depression. Yet we are discussing their use for treating anxiety. When two or more distinct mental disorders can be observed in the same person, the disorders are said to be "comorbid." There is a high rate of comorbidity for depression and anxiety. Some 59.2% of people who have a major depressive disorder also have some form of an anxiety disorder.

These comorbidity rates, as well as some other evidence, suggest a cause-and-effect relationship between depression and anxiety disorders. That relationship could exist in one of two ways. Both disorders could be caused by the same problem in the brain, or one disorder could lead to an increased vulnerability to the other. Interestingly, a 1999 study found that the increasing severity of social anxiety disorder (social phobia) increased the likelihood that major depression would develop in the patient. In fact, when major depression and anxiety disorders occur together, anxiety disorders precede major depression 67.9% of the time.

If there is a relationship between depression and anxiety, it is not surprising that certain drugs work to treat both. Ample evidence from both humans and animals suggests that the serotonergic system is altered in both types of disorders, and SSRI use is effective in the treatment of both disorders. It should be noted, however, that people who exhibit both disorders tend to be sicker for longer than those with only one disorder, and patients who have comorbid anxiety and depression do not respond as well to SSRI treatments.

MECHANISMS OF SSRIS

How do SSRI drugs work? You'll remember from Chapter 3 that neurons communicate with each other by releasing neurotransmitters into the synapse. These neurotransmitters diffuse over to the next neuron, where they bind to receptors and produce some action at the next cell through a process called synaptic transmission. Generally, it is important to stop this process quickly by removing the neurotransmitter from the synapse. There are several ways in which this removal occurs. These include: 1) The neurotransmitter simply diffuses away; 2) The neurotransmitter is broken down into inactive molecules by an enzyme; and 3) the neurotransmitter is transported back into the first cell for reuse through a process called reuptake. As is described by their name, SSRI drugs slow down the ability of the first neuron to transport serotonin out of the synapse. The net result of the drugs' action is that serotonin sits in the synaptic cleft much longer than normal, continually acting on the neighboring cell. Therefore, the short-term effect of SSRI drugs is to increase the amount of active serotonin in the brain. For several hours after taking a normal dose of an SSRI, brain serotonin levels have been shown to increase up to seven times their normal levels.

Although it is relatively clear that SSRI drugs increase active serotonin in the brain, it is not clear how these serotonin increases relate to the treatment of anxiety. Also confusing is the fact that, initially, SSRI treatment does not provide a therapeutic benefit. In fact, it can even produce symptoms of increased anxiety, including racing thoughts, agitation, and jitteriness. Often, SSRI treatment must be administered for several weeks or months before therapeutic action is observed. Increasing the dose of SSRI given does not reduce the period of delayed onset. These facts have suggested to scientists that SSRIs work in an indirect way, by making some long-term changes in receptor populations or by targeting other proteins in the brain. Although there is an abundance of research into why SSRIs are effective for treating anxiety, the mechanisms are not yet well understood.

There are several SSRIs currently being prescribed for the treatment of anxiety. Compared to the benzodiazepines and other classes of antidepressants, they are safer, causing milder side effects and fewer problems with overdose. Because they affect serotonin systems, which also play a large role in sleep patterns, the SSRIs can have effects on sleep, which vary from patient to patient. Generally, these involve a disruption of sleep patterns, but SSRIs can also cause drowsiness. All of the SSRIs are broken down in the liver.

A PROZAC TESTIMONIAL

Prozac is one of the most successful medications in the treatment of depression and anxiety. These drugs target serotonin systems and appear to have a therapeutic benefit in many mental problems that are linked to emotion. Many patients who have experienced severe anxiety found that Prozac reduced panic attacks and stabilized their moods. This testimonial was given by an employee at Emory University after taking Prozac.

> I had to get treatment because I just couldn't do regular things anymore. I couldn't sit at the movies, enjoy dinner, ride in a car, or drive. I started having strong reactions to things I could normally deal with and really didn't care about too much. I slept a lot, and I was very depressed. The way I was reacting to situations was very abnormal for me. The attacks in a way controlled me. I had to leave my full cart of groceries behind in the checkout because I just couldn't stand there. Small spaces made me cringe. I had to take the stairs, no elevators. I would also have blackouts. I couldn't drive. Ultimately when these

Although the SSRIs are very similar in action, they differ in several ways, including how tightly they bind to particular receptors on brain cells, which receptors they bind to, how quickly they work, and how quickly they are cleared from the body. For this reason, when one of these medications is not effective in treating an anxiety disorder, others will sometimes be tried and prove effective.

Paroxetine (Paxil, Paxil CR)

Paroxetine is manufactured by GlaxoSmithKline, under the brand name Paxil. It can be found in four dosings, including

attacks happened, I felt like I was underwater, completely overwhelmed and unable to interact around people with any type of control. This went on for about a year and progressively got worse until I had to get help in November of 2004. I was 27.

The doctor agreed that I had severe anxiety and I could take medicine to help it. He ran down a list of drugs of my choice, telling me all of the side effects. I could decide for myself which would be best. We both agreed on fluoxetine (20 mg), the generic Prozac. I was advised to see a therapist as well. Fluoxetine has helped me tremendously with my anxiety. Surprisingly, I felt like it started to work immediately. I only had an attack once since November and I was late taking the medication. I don't notice any changes right when I take the pill but certain side effects happen. I get headaches, I also have trouble with caffeine; the two combined give me a shooting pain in my chest (diagnosed as gas). It's much more tolerable than the anxiety, though.

10-, 20-, 30-, and 40-mg tablets. Paroxetine is also produced as a controlled-release tablet (Paxil CR) in three dosings: 12.5, 25, and 37.5 mg. Paxil is used to treat obsessive-compulsive disorder, panic disorder, generalized anxiety disorder, social anxiety disorder, and post-traumatic stress disorder. The controlled-release tablet is prescribed for panic disorder and social anxiety disorder.

Fluoxetine (Prozac)

Fluoxetine is manufactured by Eli Lilly under the name Prozac, as a 10-mg green football-shaped tablet or a 20-mg green and white capsule. It was the first SSRI introduced for the treatment of depression and anxiety disorders. Fluoxetine is prescribed for obsessive-compulsive disorder, the eating disorder bulimia nervosa, and panic disorder.

Sertraline (Zoloft)

Sertraline is manufactured by Pfizer under the name Zoloft, in three dosages: 25, 50, and 100 mg. Zoloft is prescribed for depression, obsessive-compulsive disorder, panic disorder, social anxiety disorder, and post-traumatic stress disorder. Sertraline is also used to treat obsessive-compulsive disorder in children.

Fluvoxamine (Luvox)

In the United States, fluvoxamine is only prescribed for the treatment of obsessive-compulsive disorder. It is not structurally related to the previously mentioned SSRIs, but it does have similar actions on serotonin reuptake systems. Fluvoxamine often comes in 50-mg tablets.

Escitalopram

Escitalopram is manufactured by Forest under the brand name Lexapro, and comes in a 10- or 20-mg tablet. Escitalopram is an antidepressant, but can also be prescribed for generalized anxiety disorder.

It is apparent that there are many treatments available for anxiety disorders. Care must be taken to find the best drug, both for the particular disorder as well as for the particular patient. In the next section, we discuss specific anxiety illnesses and the drugs used to treat them.

6

Alternative Therapies for Anxiety Disorders

ANTI-ANXIETY DRUGS: CONSIDERATIONS

The mood-elevating properties of the first monoamine oxidase inhibitor (MAOI) and the first tricyclic antidepressant (TCA) were discovered in the 1950s while investigating these drugs for the treatment of other ailments. By 1960, the TCA imipramine was shown to be beneficial for treating panic attacks. Because these drugs were useful in both the treatment of depression and anxiety, new antidepressants (such as the selective serotonin reuptake inhibitors) were studied for the effectiveness in treating anxiety disorders.

In 1965, the beta-blocker propranolol began to be used to treat some fear or anxiety symptoms. These drugs are particularly useful for treating panic symptoms associated with social anxiety disorder.

Over the next 20 years, the benzodiazepines, TCAs, MAOIs, and beta-blockers were used to treat anxiety disorders. By the mid-1980s, up to 10% of all Americans were taking a benzodiazepine. In 1988, fluoxetine (Prozac) was introduced by Eli Lilly as the first selective serotonin reuptake inhibitor (SSRI) for the treatment of mood and anxiety disorders. Its success led to the development of several other SSRI drugs. Today, these drugs are the first line of drug treatment for most anxiety disorders.

One continuing theme in the treatment of anxiety disorders is that there is a large amount of individual variability in the effectiveness of different treatments. Basically, this means that different things work for different people, and part of the challenge of treatment is finding the best regimen for each patient. Although this book is about the drugs used to treat anxiety disorders, it is important to recognize that education and therapy are also necessary parts of the treatment of anxiety disorder.

Cognitive-behavioral therapy has been shown to be particularly effective in treating panic disorder and phobia. In these therapy sessions, analysts carefully determine the thought processes involved in the feared situation, and help the patient practice different thought processes to overcome fear. Depending on the disorder, drugs involved, and individual, therapy can be more or less effective than drug treatment. Sometimes, the combination of both drugs and therapy can provide the best outcome. In the following sections, we look

THE PLACEBO EFFECT

The power of what a person believes should not be underestimated. Scientists have to carefully design the experiments used to determine how effective certain drugs are in the treatment of anxiety disorders. Generally, one group of patients receives the drug being tested, while another group receives an inert substance that looks like the drug. This inactive substance is called a "placebo." For a properly controlled experiment, neither the administrator nor the patient knows who is receiving the drug or placebo until the end of the experiment. As an example, some drugs that are approved for use in panic disorder have been shown to be significantly more effective than placebo in these kinds of studies, often producing a panic-free patient 50–80% of the time. However, the placebo can also be effective (although not as effective as the drug), producing a panic-free patient as much as 14–60% of the time. The placebo's therapeutic benefit comes from the patient's belief that he or she is taking something that will make him or her better, and the desire to get better.

at alternative methods for the treatment of anxiety illnesses, including the use of cognitive-behavioral therapy and other, less traditional approaches.

PSYCHOTHERAPY

Psychotherapy consists of talking to a trained mental health professional such as a psychiatrist, social worker, or clinical psychologist. In many cases, talking to a professional enables the patient to learn how to cope with anxiety. In fact, it has been shown that psychotherapy can be as effective as medication in alleviating the symptoms of most anxiety disorders.

The type of psychotherapy that has been shown to help people with anxiety problems is called "cognitive-behavioral therapy." Cognitive-behavioral therapy is the combination of two distinct kinds of psychotherapy—cognitive therapy and behavior therapy.

The *behavior* portion of the treatment helps people recognize and reduce the connection between upsetting or disturbing situations and the habitual way they react to them. Reactions such as anger, fear, depression, and other self-defeating or self-damaging behaviors are harmful to the person going through them. The behavioral component also teaches techniques to calm the mind as well as the body, so a person can feel better, think more clearly, and make better decisions.

The *cognitive* part of the therapy helps the person recognize how certain thinking patterns are causing anxiety by giving a distorted picture of what is going on in the person's life. These distorted ways of perceiving the world lead to feelings of stress and anxiety and often lead a person to make poor life decisions.

ACUPUNCTURE

The Chinese word *acupuncture* literally means "needle piercing." It is the practice of inserting very fine needles into the skin to stimulate specific points in the body, called "acupoints," for therapeutic or medicinal purposes. Practitioners of acupuncture also use heat, pressure, friction, suction, or impulses of electromagnetic energy to stimulate these acupoints. The acupoints are stimulated to balance the movement of energy (chi) in the body to restore health.

Traditional Chinese medicine considers anxiety a symptom of imbalance between the different aspects of the chi. In many cases, it can be successfully relieved by acupuncture (Figure 6.1). The acupoints used for treating anxiety are, for the most part, the same ones included in the treatment of many other types of illness, especially the relief of pain. Sometimes the relief from anxiety induced by acupuncture is very long-lasting. Many people have remained symptom-free after as few as six sessions. Others have returned for more acupuncture treatments every four to six months.

Although no one is completely certain how it works, acupuncture seems to be one of the most effective alternative treatments for anxiety disorders.

AROMATHERAPY

Aromatherapy means "treatment using scents." It is the use of essential oils from pleasant-smelling botanical oils such as lemon, lime, rose, lavender, jasmine, spearmint, and peppermint. Usually, these oils are added to bathwater or massaged directly onto the skin, but they can also be inhaled or diffused to produce scent in an entire room. It is believed that these essential oils can affect the mood, ease feelings of fatigue, reduce anxiety, and promote relaxation (Table 6.1). Aromatherapy is probably the fastest-growing area in alternative medicine. There are about 150 essential oils that are distilled from various plants, trees, and flowers. Many of these come from plants that are known to have medicinal properties. For example, peppermint has been used since the Middle Ages to treat upset stomach. Other essential oils come from plants know to be antiseptic, or pain-relieving. There are even some

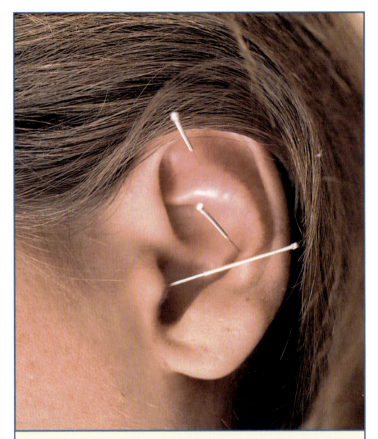

Figure 6.1 Acupuncture is the practice of inserting very fine needles into the skin to stimulate specific points in the body for therapeutic purposes. Some patients are treated with acupuncture to relieve symptoms of anxiety.

from plants that are used as antiviral agents and some from plants that have known anti-inflammatory effects. When inhaled, scents are believed to work on the brain and nervous system to bring about relaxation by stimulating the olfactory nerves. The mechanism by which these essential oils act on us is not very well understood. However, anecdotal reports suggest that they act on brain systems involved in mood and emotion. Human beings have the ability to distinguish 10,000 different smells. It is known that the perception of odors begins through stimulation of cilia (the fine hairs lining the nose) and then is relayed to the limbic system, the part of the brain that controls moods, emotions, memory, and learning. Although it is not certain how they work, studies that look at brain wave frequencies do show specific effects of particular odors. For example, smelling lavender causes increased alpha waves in the back of the head, which are associated with relaxation, while the odor of jasmine increases beta waves in the front of the head, which are associated with a more alert state.

A fragrance company in Japan conducted tests in an attempt to determine the effects of smell on people. They pumped different fragrances into an area where a number of keyboard entry operators were stationed and monitored the frequency of mistakes the workers made. The results showed that pleasant odors like jasmine and lavender were associated with significant reductions in errors.

It is known that our sense of smell can have a major effect on the way we feel. Elderly people who have lost their ability to smell are more prone to suffer from psychiatric problems such as anxiety and depression. Therefore, the continued development of this field of alternative medicine should not escape our notice.

HYPNOTISM

Hypnosis can help alleviate anxiety disorders in several ways. It can induce a state of relaxation that can directly decrease anxiety and panic. It can also be used by a therapist to help the patient focus more clearly on issues that might be causing the anxiety.

Sometimes the therapist will use fictional stories that can give the patient a new way of looking at his or her problems. Often, story telling is more useful than direct suggestions because it gives the patient a chance to accept or reject the suggestion without feeling that he or she is being controlled.

Table 6.1 Essential Oils and Their Use

OIL	USE
Basil	apathy, constipation
Bergamot	anxiety, postpartum depression, sadness
Black pepper	muscle aches
Cajeput	acne, pain, antiseptic
Chamomile	irritability, postpartum depression, stress
Cedarwood	anxiety
Clary sage	childbirth
Clove	toothaches
Cypress	varicose veins
Eucalyptus	colds
Fennel pine	nausea
Frankincense	panic attacks, insecurity, grief
Geranium	gingivitis
Ginger	muscle aches, nausea
Grapefruit	apathy
Hyssop	antiseptic
Jasmine	depression
Juniper	arthritis
Lavender	anxiety, depression, stress, panic attacks, mental fatigue, irritability, burns, asthma, arthritis

Table 6.1 *(continued)*

OIL	USE
Lemon	immune system, gingivitis
Lemongrass	dandruff
Marjoram	loneliness, constipation
Melissa-Lemonbalm	allergies
Myrrh	varicose veins
Neroli	depression, sadness, irritability, panic attacks, postpartum depression
Orange	anxiety, depression
Patchouli	warts
Peppermint	apathy, mental fatigue
Petit grain	antiseptic, depression, antibacterial
Rose	dry skin
Rosemary	poor memory, mental fatigue, grief, constipation
Sandalwood	stress, low self esteem, insecurity
Tea tree	colds, insect bites, cold sores
Thyme	hair loss
Vetiver	antibacterial, antifungal, antiseptic, sedative
Ylang ylang	low self-esteem, panic attacks

Another way that hypnosis is helpful in anxiety disorders is that it is able to produce intense concentration on a particular subject distinct from the source of anxiety or fear. For example, a person with a fear of flying may be told to imagine that he is simply going into a room to get a restful sleep when he is boarding a plane. This concentration on the nonthreatening scenario allows the person to get on a plane without experiencing feelings of anxiety.

VIRTUAL REALITY

Virtual reality uses new state-of-the-art computer graphics to put a person inside a three-dimensional virtual world. Usually this is done through the use of a very sophisticated headset that the patient wears (Figure 6.2). After putting on the headset, the person is immersed in the fabricated world, where he or she can move around and experience things as if they were actually happening. This type of therapy is particularly effective for treating phobias. For instance, Dr. Barbara Rothbaum at Emory University uses virtual reality to help people who have a fear of flying. The patient goes through everything involved in getting on an airplane, from driving to the airport, going through security, boarding the plane, and taking off and landing. The person experiences the physical sensations involved in all these things but, at the same time, realizes that it is not real. Thus, the person can rehearse the event without as much fear. All the patient's anxieties about flying can be dealt with in a "safe" setting. This has proven very effective in reducing this particular phobia. Dr. Rothbaum also uses virtual reality therapy to help people with other phobias, such as fear of crowds and heights.

BIOFEEDBACK

Biofeedback uses the idea that human beings have the ability to control the automatic functions of their bodies. For instance, a person can be trained to raise the temperature of

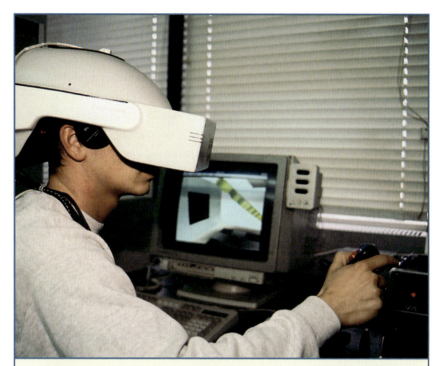

Figure 6.2 Virtual reality uses computer graphics to simulate the experience of being in a 3-D world. This type of therapy is used to treat phobias. By wearing a headset and entering a virtual world, patients can come face-to-face with their fears while remaining in a safe environment.

one hand, without contracting the hand muscles, 5 to 10°F (10 to 15°C) higher than that of the other hand. Even laboratory animals can be taught to do this. Rats can be trained to produce different temperatures in each of their two ears in order to obtain a food reward.

Biofeedback has been shown to have many beneficial uses. One example is the use of biofeedback to curtail the pain of migraine headaches. People trained in biofeedback can divert blood to their heads and arms and cause their hands to quickly become warmer than normal. This can effectively ease a migraine because it reduces the amount of blood in the blood vessels of the head. Biofeedback can also be used to train people to block the pain of colitis, neuritis, and other conditions. Many of these techniques have been scientifically verified.

Biofeedback uses a special machine and sensors to record muscle contractions and skin temperature. The machine can tell the person what affect his or her concentration is having on things like blood flow and body temperature. Eventually, the person can recognize and manage these responses on his or her own.

Once viewed with skepticism, the deliberate control of "involuntary" responses is now seen to be effective in the treatment of migraine headaches and asthma. It can also be used to help people control the autonomic or bodily responses that they experience during panic attacks.

MEDITATION: MIND-BODY THERAPY

Meditation is a simple way to safely balance a person's physical, emotional, and mental states. It has been shown to reduce activity in the nervous system. This is the function of the parasympathetic branch of the autonomic or involuntary nervous system. More and more doctors are prescribing meditation as a way to relax from the everyday stresses of life (Figure 6.3).

The use of meditation is not new. Meditative techniques exist in the traditions of many of the world's great religions. In fact, practically all religious groups practice meditation in one form or another, although Buddhism, practiced widely in eastern and central Asia, is perhaps the best known. Buddhists believe that meditation gets us in touch with our unconscious minds and makes it possible to live life to its fullest potential.

Only during the past three decades has scientific study focused on the clinical effects of meditation on health. During the 1960s, it was reported that meditation masters in India could perform extraordinary acts of bodily control when they were in altered states of consciousness. These reports captured

Figure 6.3 Meditation is an introspective process that balances a person's mental, physical, and emotional states by reducing activity in the nervous system. Many doctors prescribe meditation as a way to relax from daily stresses.

the interest of Western researchers who were searching for alternatives to traditional medicine for controlling many of the psychological aspects of disease.

There are various types of meditation: Prayer is probably the best known, but there is also TM (transcendental meditation), mindfulness meditation, and, from the Eastern tradition, Zen meditation, Buddhist meditation, and Taoist meditation. All of these types of meditation focus on quieting the busy mind. The intent is not to remove stimulation but rather to direct the concentration toward one healing element—one sound, one word, one image, or the pattern of the breath. When the mind is "filled" with the feeling of calm and peace, it becomes distracted from focusing on troubling or disturbing things.

The simplest form of concentrative meditation is to sit quietly and pay attention to your breathing. Focusing the mind on the continuous rhythm of breathing in and breathing out provides a natural object of meditation. As you focus your awareness on breathing, the mind becomes captivated by the rhythm of inhalation and exhalation. As a result, breathing becomes more regular and the mind becomes more tranquil and aware.

There are many ways, other than the use of anti-anxiety drugs, to control the symptoms of anxiety. Although some of these methods may be outside the mainstream of modern medicine, many of them are gaining respect as viable alternatives to the use of drugs.

7

Teenagers and Anti-Anxiety Drugs

Anxiety affects people of all ages. Even though adults, adolescents, and children have different sources of stress in their lives, those stressors produce similar effects on the body, regardless of age. For adolescents, school, peer groups, parents, moving, and health can all be sources of stress that cause anxiety. In some cases, this may lead to many of the anxiety disorders that we have discussed in this book. If left untreated, people with these anxiety disorders are more likely to perform poorly in school, have stunted social development, and abuse drugs.

Anxiety disorders affect up to 17% of adolescents. Although symptoms of teenage anxiety often look similar to the same illness in adults, at other times, it manifests in different ways. Parents may find their teens unmanageable at home and school, which may be a manifestation of the young adult's response to the stressors in their lives. In other situations, anxiety may show up as demanding, attention-seeking behavior. These symptoms do not mean someone has an anxiety disorder, but they may be warning signs.

Anxiety disorders often lead to poor performance in school for several reasons. Problems with anxiety are sometimes associated with learning disorders and difficulty concentrating. Teens who have anxiety disorders often withdraw from social groups as well as their studies, and may avoid school altogether.

As with adults, anxiety disorders in adolescence are often accompanied by other mental illnesses. Many teens develop more than one anxiety disorder. There is also a significant comorbidity with depression; 60 to 80% of depressed children and adolescents also suffer from an anxiety disorder. Anxiety disorders are also strongly associated with eating disorders. Like adults, young people who suffer from multiple mental illnesses are often less responsive to drug treatment.

HISTORY OF ANXIETY DISORDERS IN CHILDREN AND ADOLESCENTS

Before 1980, there weren't many references to childhood or adolescent anxiety in the psychiatric literature. But in 1980, three categories of anxiety disorder were defined, in the third edition of the *Diagnostic and Statistical Manual of Mental Disorders* (DSM-III). These categories were disorders that developed in infancy, childhood, or adolescence. DSM-III also recognized that other anxiety disorders, such as panic disorder, PTSD, and OCD, could also develop in childhood.

Before the idea of anxiety disorders in children was established, studies tended to focus on behaviors that suggested an anxiety disorder. Much research prior to 1980 investigated the effects of certain medications on children and teens who refused to go to school. This refusal could be rooted in several types of disorders, including phobia, social anxiety disorder, and depression.

The earliest studies on the treatment of anxiety in non-adults focused mainly on children rather than adolescents. In the 1960s, chlordiazepoxide (librium), a benzodiazepine, was suggested as an effective treatment for several emotional problems in children, including helping children who wouldn't go to school. Although a couple of other drugs were used to treat childhood anxiety, including diphenhydramine and phenobarital, there is very little historical literature investigating the treatment of childhood anxiety disorders. Historically, the mechanisms by which these drugs worked were unknown.

SUBSTANCE ABUSE

Teenagers with anxiety, like adults, are more likely to abuse drugs. Sometimes this involves drinking alcohol, but more often, anxiety-ridden teens try to self-medicate with marijuana. These individuals report that marijuana calms their symptoms of anxiety, and so they use it regularly. Teens who use marijuana often will experience symptoms of withdrawal when they do not use the drug, including nervousness and irritability—the same symptoms produced by their anxiety disorders. This makes these teens more sensitive to marijuana withdrawal, and they will use more marijuana to avoid the

ANTIDEPRESSANTS AND SUICIDE

In 2004, the Food and Drug Administration (FDA) issued a warning about the use of antidepressant drugs in children and adolescents. Several studies that investigated the use of nine different antidepressant drugs in children and adolescents with major depression or anxiety disorders found that there was a 4% risk of suicidal thinking and behavior, a significant increase over the 2% risk of suicidal thoughts and behavior in subjects who received a placebo. No suicides actually occurred in the experiments. Based on these data, the FDA now requires that the following warnings be included when an antidepressant drug is purchased for children or adolescents: "Antidepressants increase the risk of suicidal thinking and behavior in children and adolescents with major depression or other psychiatric disorders. Anyone considering the use of an antidepressant in a child or adolescent must balance the risk of increased suicidal thinking and behavior with clinical need. Children and adolescents who are started on antidepressant therapy should be closely monitored for clinical worsening, suicidal thinking and behavior, or unusual behavioral changes. Families and caregivers should be part of the monitoring process and communicate with the prescribing physician."

withdrawal symptoms. Marijuana affects memory and attention, which has detrimental effects on school performance. Importantly, marijuana can also decrease the effectiveness of some drugs that are used to treat anxiety disorders.

TREATMENT OF ADOLESCENT ANXIETY

There are several strategies for helping adolescents with anxiety disorders. Although medications can be effective to help control anxiety symptoms, they are not a long-term solution. Instead, it is recommended that therapists and physicians help the affected teens learn how to control their anxiety.

The major classes of drugs used for adolescent anxiety are the same used to treat these disorders in adults. They include antidepressants, benzodiazepines, and buspirone. Although antidepressants are often the first line of drug treatment for anxiety disorders (as they are in adults), there is evidence that these drugs may increase suicidal thinking and behavior in some children and adolescents. The SSRIs have been shown to help treat adolescent OCD, social anxiety disorder, generalized anxiety, and panic disorder, and are often used as drug treatment for these conditions. The risks must be weighed with the benefits and the afflicted individuals should be monitored closely.

Research into the treatment of adolescent anxiety disorders is still in the early stages. Few studies have been conducted (compared with those regarding adults) on the effectiveness of anti-anxiety drugs in adolescents. However, as the use of these drugs continues to rise, the growing interest will continue to encourage further research into this area.

CONCLUSION

The prevalence of anxiety disorders has spurred the search for pharmacological ways to treat these pathologies. To date, doctors have found that drugs from two broad classes—the benzodiazepines and selective serotonin reuptake inhibitors, or SSRIs—are the most effective ways to treat anxiety-based illnesses. However, the search for drugs that will have precise effects on particular anxiety illnesses is still going on in many research laboratories across the United States, Canada, and Europe. Every year, more and more is understood about the specific brain regions that govern the expression of fear and anxiety, and more details about the neurochemistry of these regions are obtained. The search for knowledge in this area is one of the most exciting and potentially one of the most rewarding challenges for modern neuroscience.

Glossary

Amygdala—Brain region responsible for coordinating the response to fear and anxiety.

Barbiturate—An acid derivative that acts as a central nervous system depressant and is used as a sedative.

Benzodiazepine—A drug used to treat anxiety disorders by increasing the ability of the neurotransmitter GABA to inhibit cells in the brain.

Beta-blocker—Drug that suppresses the autonomic stress response that causes fear-like symptoms brought on by social anxiety disorder.

Antidepressant—A drug used to relieve or prevent depression.

Anxiety disorder—Any of various disorders in which anxiety is either the primary disturbance or is the result of confronting a feared situation or object.

Behavioral therapy—Working with a therapist to try to reduce fear of an object or situation through the use of particular exercises.

Central gray—A region deep in the brain that suppresses motor activation and causes freezing behavior.

Cerebral cortex—The thinking areas of the brain.

Dopamine—A monoamine neurotransmitter formed in the brain and essential for the normal functioning of the central nervous system.

Extinction—The natural process by which exposure to a feared object in a safe environment reduces fear of that object over time.

GABA—An inhibitory neurotransmitter in the brain that acts to reduce the activity or firing rate of neurons.

Generalized anxiety disorder (**GAD**)—Psychological disorder marked by long-term worry.

Hypothalamus—A region at the base of the brain, just above the brain stem, that controls changes in blood pressure, pupil dilation, heart rate, and the release of stress hormones into the bloodstream.

Innate—Referring to something that humans are born with.

Neurotransmitter—A chemical substance, such as acetylcholine or dopamine, that transmits nerve impulses across a synapse.

Norepinephrine (also called **noradrenaline**)—Controls emotional arousal and increases attention.

Obsessive-compulsive disorder (**OCD**)—A condition marked by constant intrusive thoughts and irresistible time-consuming behaviors.

Operant conflict test—A test conducted on an animal or human in which the subject must perform a task to obtain a specific result. Something that the animal likes or needs (such as food or water) is used as positive reinforcement to teach a task.

Panic attack—An extreme physical response to stress and fear. Symptoms include shortness of breath, increased heart rate, chest pain, dizziness, choking sensations, numbness or tingling, hot/cold flashes, sweating, trembling, and nausea. Victims of these episodes feel an intense fear that can be better characterized as terror, often of losing control of their body and/or mind, and thoughts of death.

Panic disorder—A psychological disorder characterized by the repeated and often unpredictable occurrence of panic attacks.

Phobia—An inappropriately intense and irrational fear toward some object or situation.

Post-traumatic stress disorder (**PTSD**)—Occurs following the experience of a severe threat to life or physical well-being.

Recticular net—A brain stem region that accentuates the reflex response to a sudden loud noise that results in an increased startle reaction.

Serotonin—An organic compound formed from tryptophan and found in animal and human tissue, especially the brain, blood serum, and gastric mucous membranes, and active in vasoconstriction, stimulation of the smooth muscles, transmission of impulses between nerve cells, and regulation of cyclic body processes.

Social anxiety disorder (also called social phobia)—Fear of doing something wrong and being embarrassed in front of other people.

Bibliography

Books

Charney, D. S., and E. J. Nestler. *Neurobiology of Mental Illness.* New York: Oxford University Press, 2004.

Cooper, J. R., F. E. Bloom, and R. H. Roth. *The Biochemical Basis of Neuropharmacology.* New York: Oxford University Press, 2003.

Julian, R. M. *A Primer of Drug Action: A Concise, Nontechnical Guide to the Actions, Uses, and Side Effects of Psychoactive Drugs.* New York: W. H. Freeman and Company, 1995.

Morrison, A. L. *The Antidepressant Sourcebook, A User's Guide for Patients and Families.* New York: Doubleday, 1999.

PDR Drug Guide for Mental Health Professionals. Montvale: Thomson PDR, 2004.

Rosenweig, M. R., A. L. Leiman, and S. M. Breedlove. *Biological Pyschology.* Sunderland: Sinauer Associates, Inc., 1999.

Articles

"Anxiety Disorders." NIMH Website. Available online at *http://www.nimh. nih.gov/HealthInformation/anxietymenu.cfm.*

Belzer, K., and F. R. Schneier. "Comorbidity of Anxiety and Depressive Disorders: Issues in Conceptualization, Assessment, and Treatment." *Journal of Psychiatric Practice* 10(5) (2004): 296–306.

Berle, D., and V. Starcevic. "Thought-action Fusion: Review of the Literature and Future Directions." *Clinical Psychology Review* 25(3) (2005): 263–84.

Berrios, G. "Anxiety Disorders, A Conceptual History." *Journal of Affective Disorders* 56 (1999): 83–94.

Brunello, N., P. Blier, L. L. Judd, J. Mendlewisz, C. J. Nelson, D. Souery, J. Zohar, and G. Racagni. "Noradrenaline in Mood and Anxiety Disorders: Basic and Clinical Studies." *International Clinical Psychopharmacology* 18(4) (2003): 191–202.

Davidson, J. R. T., D. J. Stein , A. Y. Shalev, and R. Yehuda. "Posttraumatic Stress Disorder: Acquisition, Recognition, Course, and Treatment." *Journal of Neuropsychiatry and Clinical Neuroscience* 16 (2004): 137–147.

Diler, R. S. "Panic Disorder in Children and Adolescents." *Yonsei Medical Journal* 44(1) (2003): 174–179.

Garland, E. J. "Rages and Refusals: Managing the Many Faces of Adolescent Anxiety." *Canadian Family Physician* 47 (2001): 1023–1030.

Goodman, W. K. "Selecting Pharmacotherapy for Generalized Anxiety Disorder." *Journal of Clinical Psychiatry* 65 Suppl. 13 (2005): 8–13.

Handley, S. L. "5-Hydroxytryptamine Pathways in Anxiety and Its Treatment." *Pharmacology and Therapeutics* 66 (1995): 103–148.

Heuzenroeder, L., M. Donnelly, M. M. Haby, C. Mihalopoulos, R. Rossell, R. Carter, G. Andrews, and T. Vos. "Cost-effectiveness of Psychological and Pharmacological Interventions for Generalized Anxiety Disorder and Panic Disorder." *Australian and New Zealand Journal of Psychiatry* 38 (2004): 602–612.

"History of Anxiety Disorders." HealthyPlace Website. Available online at *http://www.healthyplace.com/communities/anxiety/paems/panic/history_anxiety_disorders.htm.*

Jacobs, B., and E. Azmitia. "Structure and Function of the Brain Serotonin System." *Physiological Reviews* 72(1) (1992): 165–229.

Kasper, S., and E. Resinger. "Panic Disorder: The Place of Benzodiazepines and Selective Serotonin Reuptake Inhibitors." *European Neuropsychopharmacology* 11 (2001): 307–321.

Kessler, R. C., P. Berglund, O. Demler, R. Jin, D. Koretz, K. R. Merikangas, A. J. Rush, E. E. Walters, and P. S. Wang. "The Epidemiology of Major Depressive Disorder: Results From the National Comorbidity Survey Replication (NCS-R)." *Journal of the American Medical Association* 289(23) (2003): 3095–3105.

Kessler, R. C., P. Stang, H. U. Wittchen, M. Stein, and E. E. Walters. "Lifetime Co-morbidities Between Social Phobia and Mood Disorders in the US National Comorbidity Survey." *Psychological Medicine* 29(3) (1999): 555–567.

Ledoux, J. E. "Emotional Circuits in the Brain." *Annual Review of Neuroscience* 23 (2000):155–184.

Lepine, J. P. "The Epidemiology of Anxiety Disorders: Prevalence, and Societal Costs." *Journal of Clinical Psychiatry* 63(Suppl. 14) (2002): 4–8.

Milan, M. J. "The Neurobiology and Control of Anxious States" *Progress in Neurobiology* 70 (2003): 83–244.

Nemeroff, C. B. "Anxiolytics: Past, Present, and Future Agents." *Journal of Clinical Psychiatry* 64(Suppl. 3) (2003): 3–6.

O'Donnell, T., K.M. Hegadoren, and N. C. Coupland. "Noradrenergic Mechanisms in the Pathophysiology of Post-traumatic Stress Disorder." *Biological Psychiatry* 50 (2004): 273–283.

Pincus, H. A., M. A. Tanielian, S. C. Marcus, M. Olfson, D. A. Zarin, M. D. Thompson, and J. M. Zito. "Prescribing Trends in Psychotropic Medications." *Journal of the American Medical Association* 279(7) (1998): 526–531.

Bibliography

Rynn, M. A., and O. Brawman-Mintzer. "Generalized Anxiety Disorder: Acute and Chronic Treatment." CNS Spectr. 9(10) (2004): 716–23.

Schruers K., K. Koning, J. Luermans, M. J. Haack, and E. Griez. "Obsessive-compulsive Disorder: A Critical Review of Therapeutic Perspectives." *Acta Psychiatrica Scandinavica* 111(4)(2005): 261–71.

Uphouse, L. "Multiple Serotonin Receptors: Too Many, Not Enough, or Just the Right Number?" *Neuroscience and Biobehavioral Reviews* 21(5) (1997): 679–698.

Westenberg, H.G.M., and M. R. Liebowitz. "Overview of Panic and Social Anxiety Disorders." *Journal of Clinical Psychiatry* 65(Suppl. 14) (2004): 22–26.

Yamada, M., and H. Yasuhara. "Clinical Pharmacology of MAO Inhibitors: Safety and Future." *Neurotoxicology* 25 (2004): 215–221.

Zohar, J., and H. G. M. Westenberg. "Anxiety Disorders: A Review of Tricyclic Antidepressants and Selective Serotonin Reuptake Inhibitors." *Acta Psychiatrica Scandinavica* 101(Suppl. 403) (2000): 39–49.

Julian, R. M. *A Primer of Drug Action: A Concise, Nontechnical Guide to the Actions, Uses, and Side Effects of Psychoactive Drugs.* New York: W. H. Freeman and Company, 1995.

Ledoux, J. *The Emotional Brain: The Mysterious Underpinnings of Emotional Life.* New York: Simon & Schuster, 1995.

Morrison, A. L. *The Antidepressant Sourcebook, A User's Guide for Patients and Families.* New York: Doubleday, 1999.

Rachman, S. *Anxiety* Hove: Psychology Press: New York: Taylor and Francis, 2004.

Restak, R. M. *Poe's Heart and the Mountain Climber: Exploring the Effect of Anxiety on Our Brains and Our Culture.* New York: Harmony Books, 2004.

Warner, J. *Perfect Madness: Motherhood in the Age of Anxiety.* New York: Riverhead Books, 2005.

Websites

http://www.adaa.org/
Anxiety Disorders Association of America

http://www.healthyplace.com/communities/anxiety/paems/panic/
history_anxiety_disorders.htm
HealthyPlace.com

www.nimh.nih.gov/HealthInformation/anxietymenu.cfm
National Institute of Mental Health.

http://www.baltimorepsych.com/anxiety.htm
Northern County Psychiatric Associates

http://www.rcpsych.ac.uk/info/factsheets/pfacanti.asp
Royal College of Psychiatrists in the United Kingdom

http://www.mentalhealth.samhsa.gov/publications/allpubs/
ken98-0045/default.asp
United States Department of Health and Human Services

Index

Index

Picture Credits

Trademarks

About the Authors

Sayamwong Hammack "Jom" earned his Ph.D. from the University of Colorado studying how the serotonin system is altered in the learned helplessness model, which produces an anxiety-like state. He continues to research serotonin influences on anxiety in his current position as a postdoctoral fellow at Emory University. His work has been published in such journals as *The Journal of Neuroscience, Neuroscience,* and *Behavioral Neuroscience.* He currently lives in Atlanta, Georgia, with his wife, Heather. He would like to dedicate his contribution to this book to his parents.

Donna Toufexis completed her doctoral training in neuroendocrinology at McGill University in Montreal, Canada, and postdoctoral training at Concordia University in Montreal. Toufexis is presently a research associate at the Center for Behavioral Neuroscience (CBN) at Emory University in Atlanta. Her primary research interest is the characterization of brain mechanisms that govern fear and anxiety. In particular, Toufexis is interested in the role that neuroactive hormones estrogen, testosterone, and oxytocin play in the regulation of fear and anxiety.

About the Editor

David J. Triggle is a University Professor and a Distinguished Professor in the School of Pharmacy and Pharmaceutical Sciences at the State University of New York at Buffalo. He studied in the United Kingdom and earned his B.Sc. degree in Chemistry from the University of Southampton and a Ph.D. degree in Chemistry at the University of Hull. Following post-doctoral work at the University of Ottawa in Canada and the University of London in the United Kingdom, he assumed a position at the School of Pharmacy at Buffalo. He served as Chairman of the Department of Biochemical Pharmacology from 1971 to 1985 and as Dean of the School of Pharmacy from 1985 to 1995. From 1995 to 2001 he served as the Dean of the Graduate School, and as the University Provost from 2000 to 2001. He is the author of several books dealing with the chemical pharmacology of the autonomic nervous system and drug-receptor interactions, some 400 scientific publications, and has delivered over 1,000 lectures worldwide on his research.